# the AMAZING SPIDER-MAN



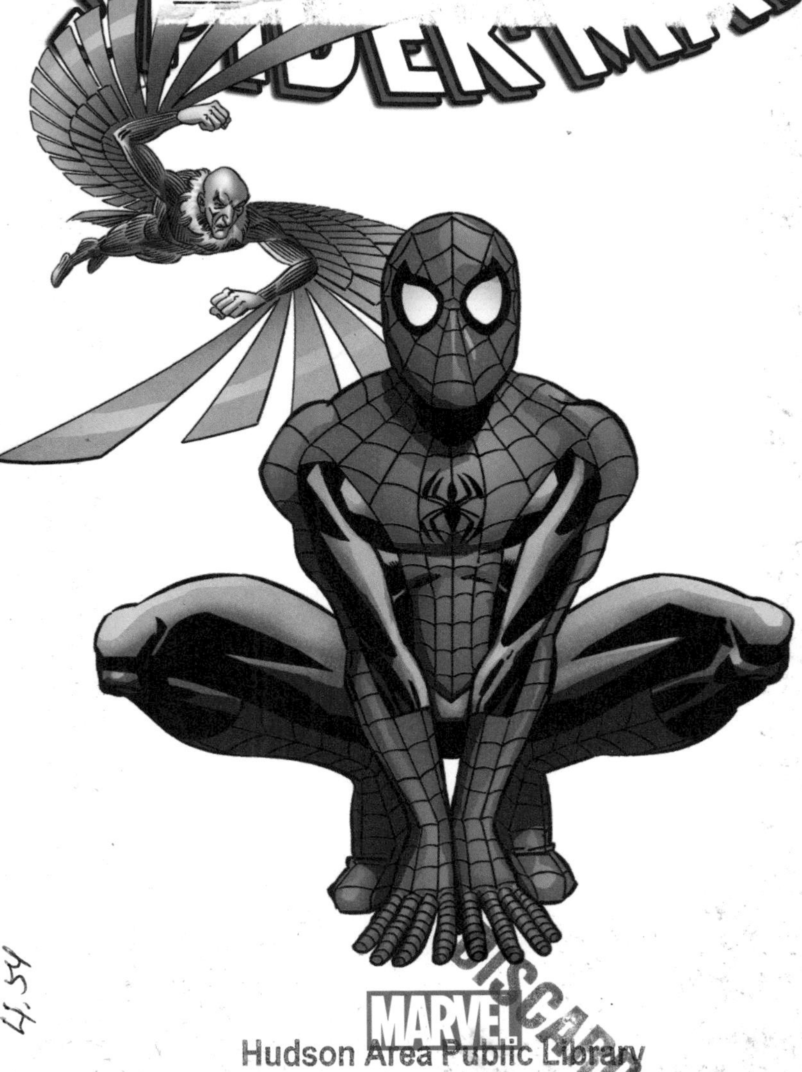



MARVEL

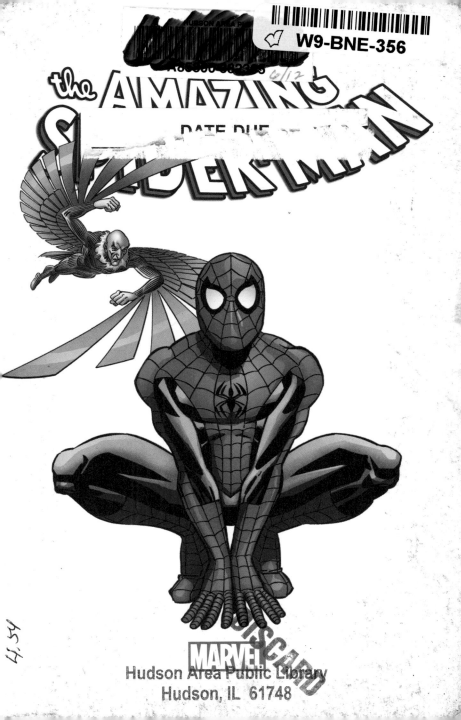

**AMAZING SPIDER-MAN VOL. 2: THE VULTURE.** First printing 2012. ISBN# 978-0-7851-6476-0. Published by MARVEL WORLDWIDE, INC., a subsidiary of MARVEL ENTERTAINMENT, LLC. OFFICE OF PUBLICATION: 135 West 50th Street, New York, NY 10020. Copyright © 2012 Marvel Characters, Inc. All rights reserved. $6.99 per copy in the U.S. and $7.99 in Canada (GST #R127032852); Canadian Agreement #40668537. All characters featured in this issue and the distinctive names and likenesses thereof, and all related indicia are trademarks of Marvel Characters, Inc. No similarity between any of the names, characters, persons, and/or institutions in this magazine with those of any living or dead person or institution is intended, and any such similarity which may exist is purely coincidental. **Printed in the U.S.A.** ALAN FINE, EVP - Office of the President, Marvel Worldwide, Inc. and EVP & CMO Marvel Characters B.V.; DAN BUCKLEY, Publisher & President - Print, Animation & Digital Divisions; JOE QUESADA, Chief Creative Officer; TOM BREVOORT, SVP of Publishing; DAVID BOGART, SVP of Operations & Procurement, Publishing; RUWAN JAYATILLEKE, SVP & Associate Publisher, Publishing; C.B. CEBULSKI, SVP of Creator & Content Development; DAVID GABRIEL, SVP of Publishing Sales & Circulation; MICHAEL PASCIULLO, SVP of Brand Planning & Communications; JIM O'KEEFE, VP of Operations & Logistics; DAN CARR, Executive Director of Publishing Technology; SUSAN CRESPI, Editorial Operations Manager; ALEX MORALES, Publishing Operations Manager; STAN LEE, Chairman Emeritus. For information regarding advertising in Marvel Comics or on Marvel.com, please contact John Dokes, SVP Integrated Sales and Marketing, at jdokes@marvel.com. For Marvel subscription inquiries, please call 800-217-9158. **Manufactured between 4/23/2012 and 5/21/2012 by SHERIDAN BOOKS, INC., CHELSEA, MI, USA.**

10 9 8 7 6 5 4 3 2 1

# THE VULTURE

Writer
## JOE CARAMAGNA
Comic Artists
## FRANCESCA CIREGIA & ELENA CASAGRANDE
Colorist
## SOTOCOLOR
Letterer
## JOE CARAMAGNA
Cover Artists
## PATRICK SCHERBERGER with EDGAR DELGADO
Spot Illustrations
## SCOTT KOBLISH with SOTOCOLOR
and **PAUL RYAN, JOHN ROMITA & DAMION SCOTT**
Assistant Editor
## MICHAEL HORWITZ
Comic Editors
## NATHAN COSBY & JORDAN D. WHITE
Prose Editor
## CORY LEVINE

Assistant Editors: Alex Starbuck & Nelson Ribeiro
Editors, Special Projects: Jennifer Grünwald & Mark D. Beazley
Senior Editor, Special Projects: Jeff Youngquist
Senior Vice President of Sales: David Gabriel
Associate Publisher & SVP of Print, Animation and Digital Media: Ruwan Jayatilleke
SVP of Brand Planning & Communications: Michael Pasciullo
Book Design: Marie Drion & Joe Frontirre
Editor In Chief: Axel Alonso
Chief Creative Officer: Joe Quesada
Publisher: Dan Buckley
Executive Producer: Alan Fine

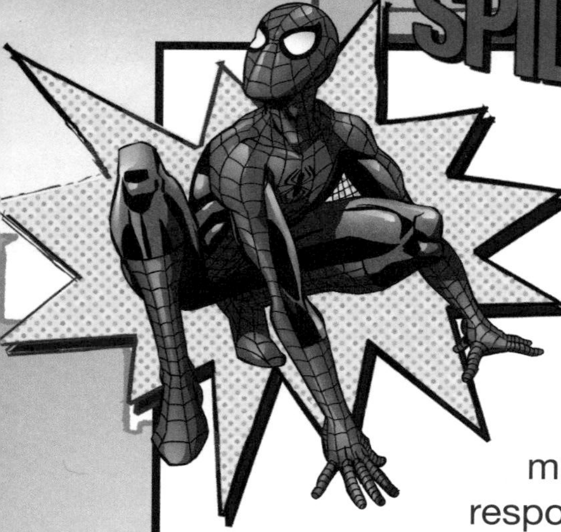

## SPIDER-MAN

The former professional wrestler turned super hero learned the hard way that with great power must come great responsibility. To make up for his past mistakes, he has vowed to protect New York City from all those who wish to do harm.

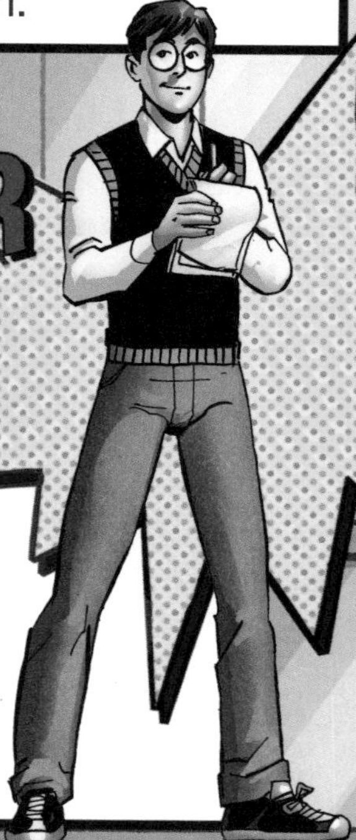

## PETER PARKER

Raised from childhood by his Uncle Ben and Aunt May, he always dreamed of becoming a scientist like his late father. But after a lab accident — and a radioactive spider bite — granted him special powers, he discovered his true calling.

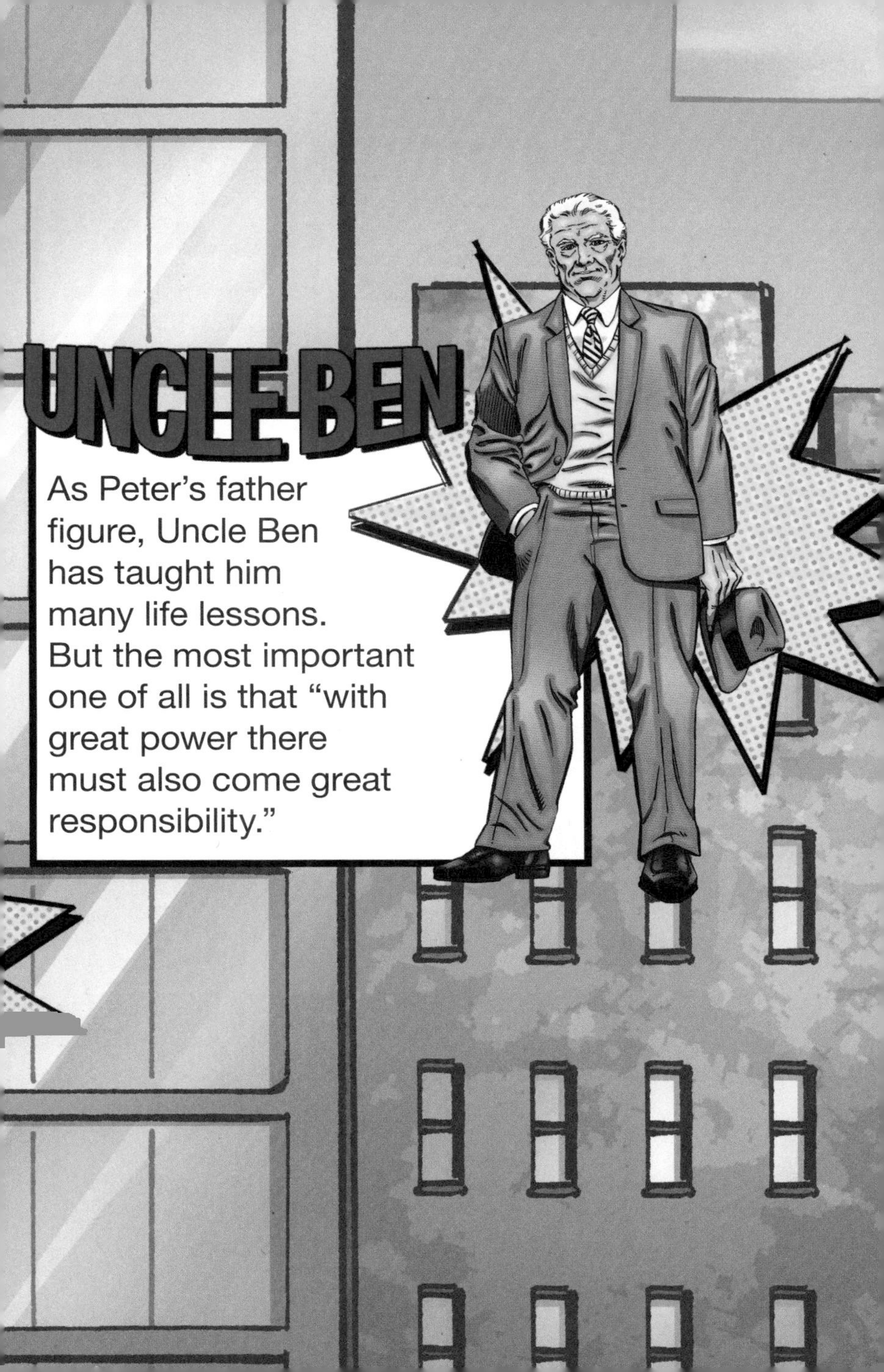

# UNCLE BEN

As Peter's father figure, Uncle Ben has taught him many life lessons. But the most important one of all is that "with great power there must also come great responsibility."

# AUNT MAY

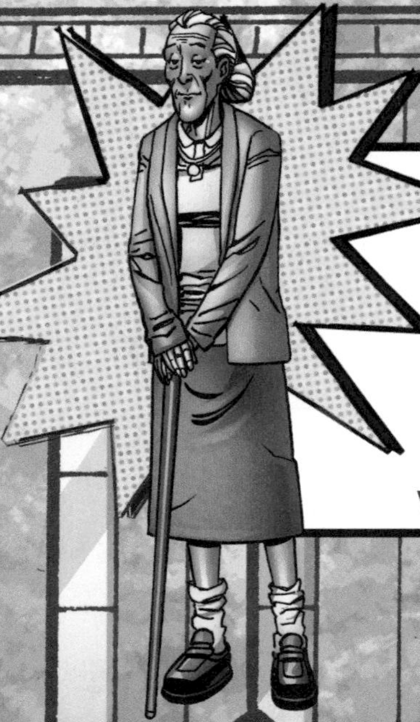

After the death of Peter's parents, May Parker and her husband, Ben, raised their nephew as if he were their own child.

# FLASH THOMPSON

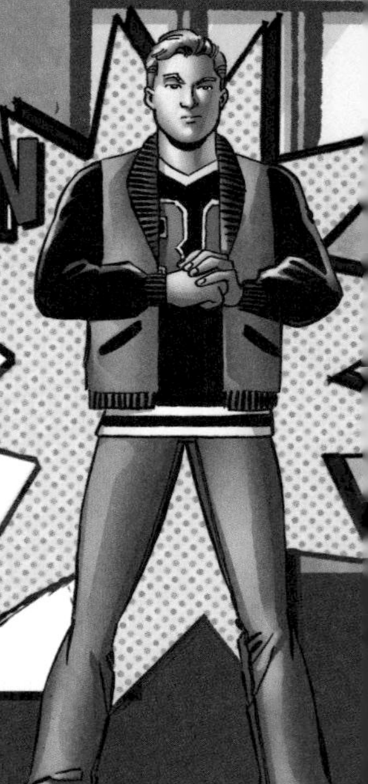

Eugene "Flash" Thompson is Midtown High's star football player but also its biggest bully. Little does he know his favorite victim, Peter Parker, is really New York City's greatest super hero!

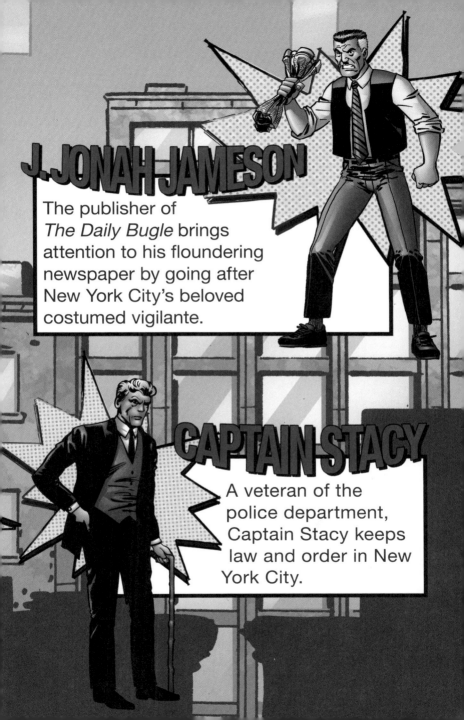

## J. JONAH JAMESON

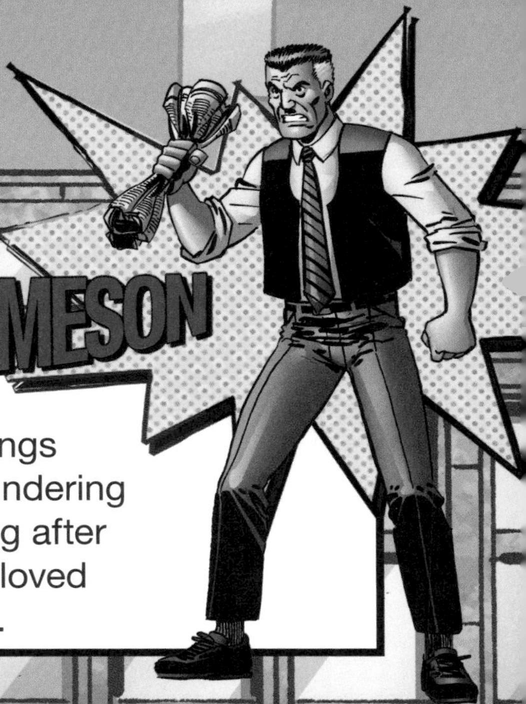

The publisher of *The Daily Bugle* brings attention to his floundering newspaper by going after New York City's beloved costumed vigilante.

## CAPTAIN STACY

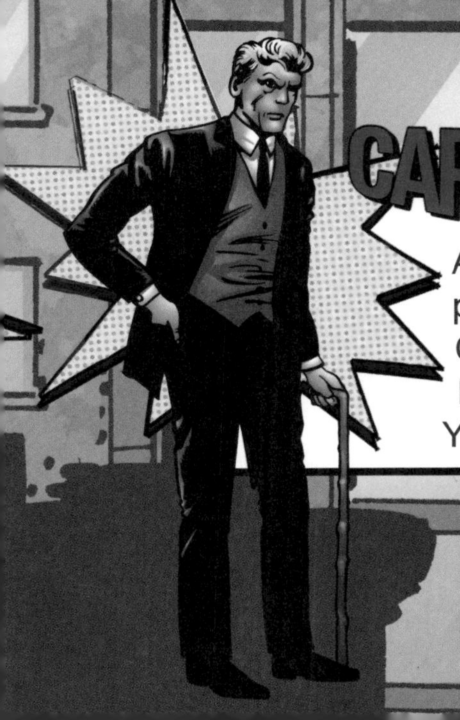

A veteran of the police department, Captain Stacy keeps law and order in New York City.

# THE VULTURE

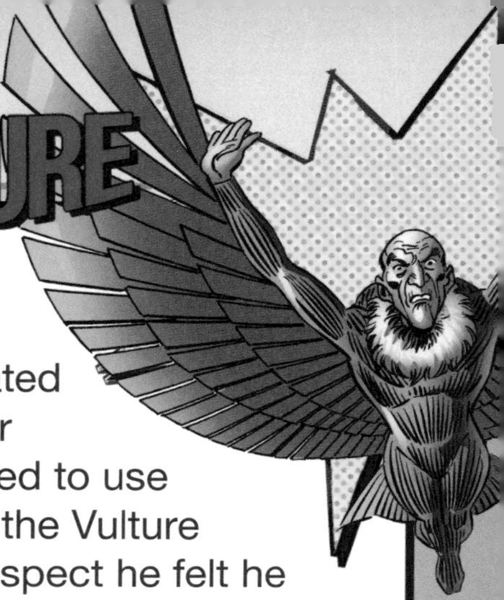

Adrian Toomes spent his life as an engineer but never felt appreciated by his employers. After he was fired, he decided to use his greatest invention, the Vulture harness, to gain the respect he felt he always deserved.

# SANDMAN

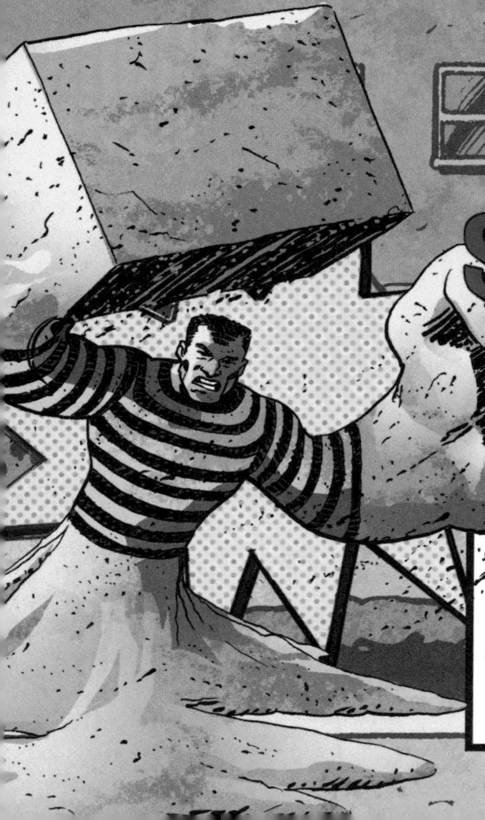

While on the run from the police, a chemical accident left criminal Flint Marko with the ability to turn his body into sand.

# DOCTOR OCTOPUS

Dr. Otto Octavius is a world-renowned, yet accident-prone, nuclear physicist. After one accident too many left him melded to a set of four mechanical arms, he became Spider-Man's most formidable super villain!

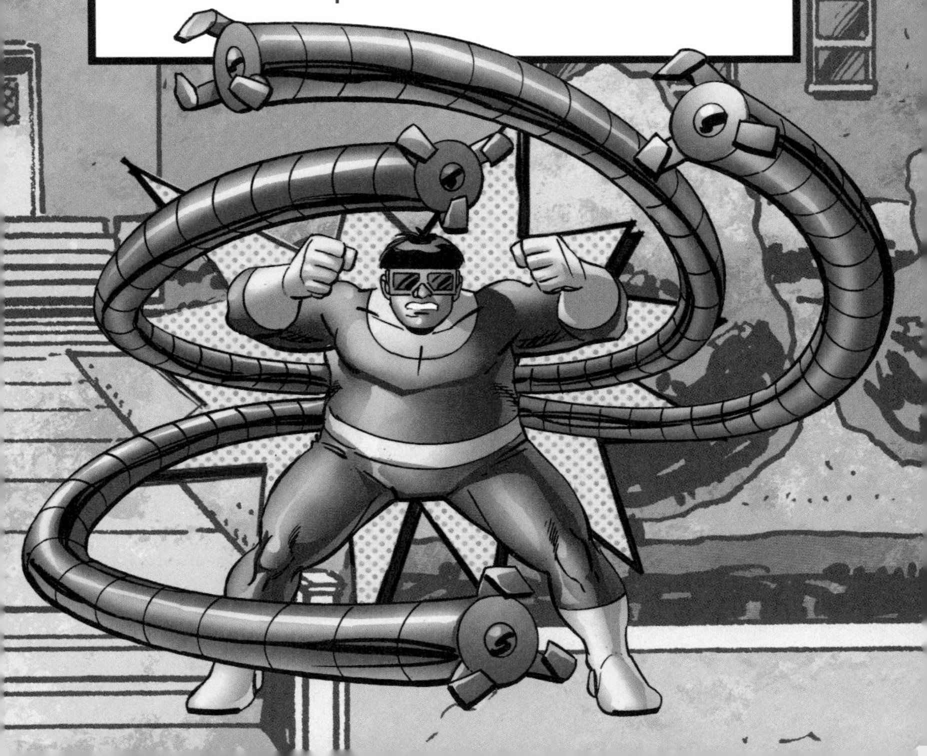

# GREEN GOBLIN

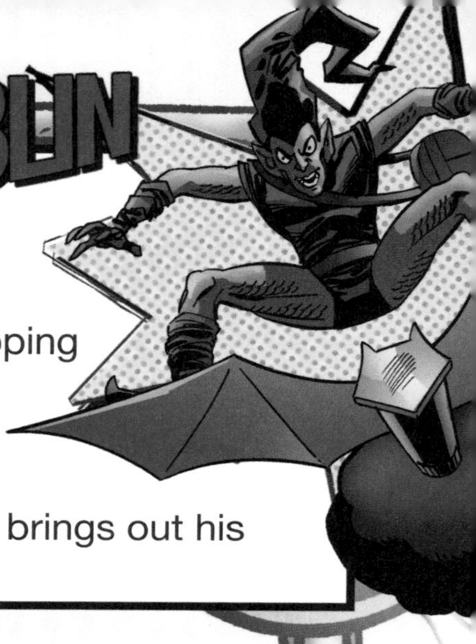

Norman Osborn is a military contractor who was tasked with developing a super-soldier serum. But aside from extraordinary abilities, his flawed formula also brings out his devilish dark side!

# KRAVEN THE HUNTER

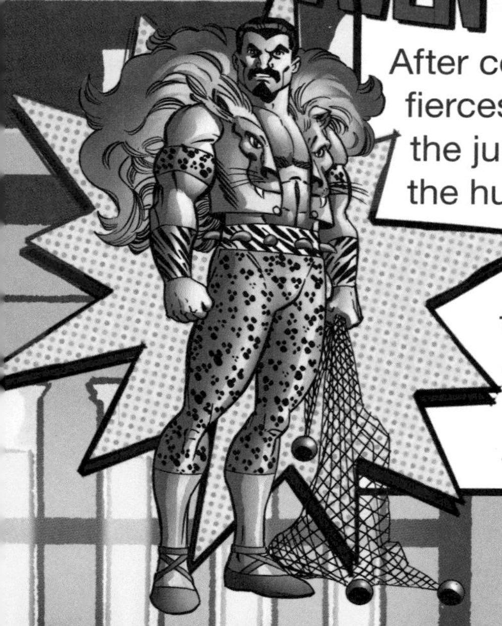

After conquering the fiercest animals in all the jungles of Africa, the hunter Sergei Kravinoff set his sights on the most elusive game of them all: the Amazing Spider-Man!

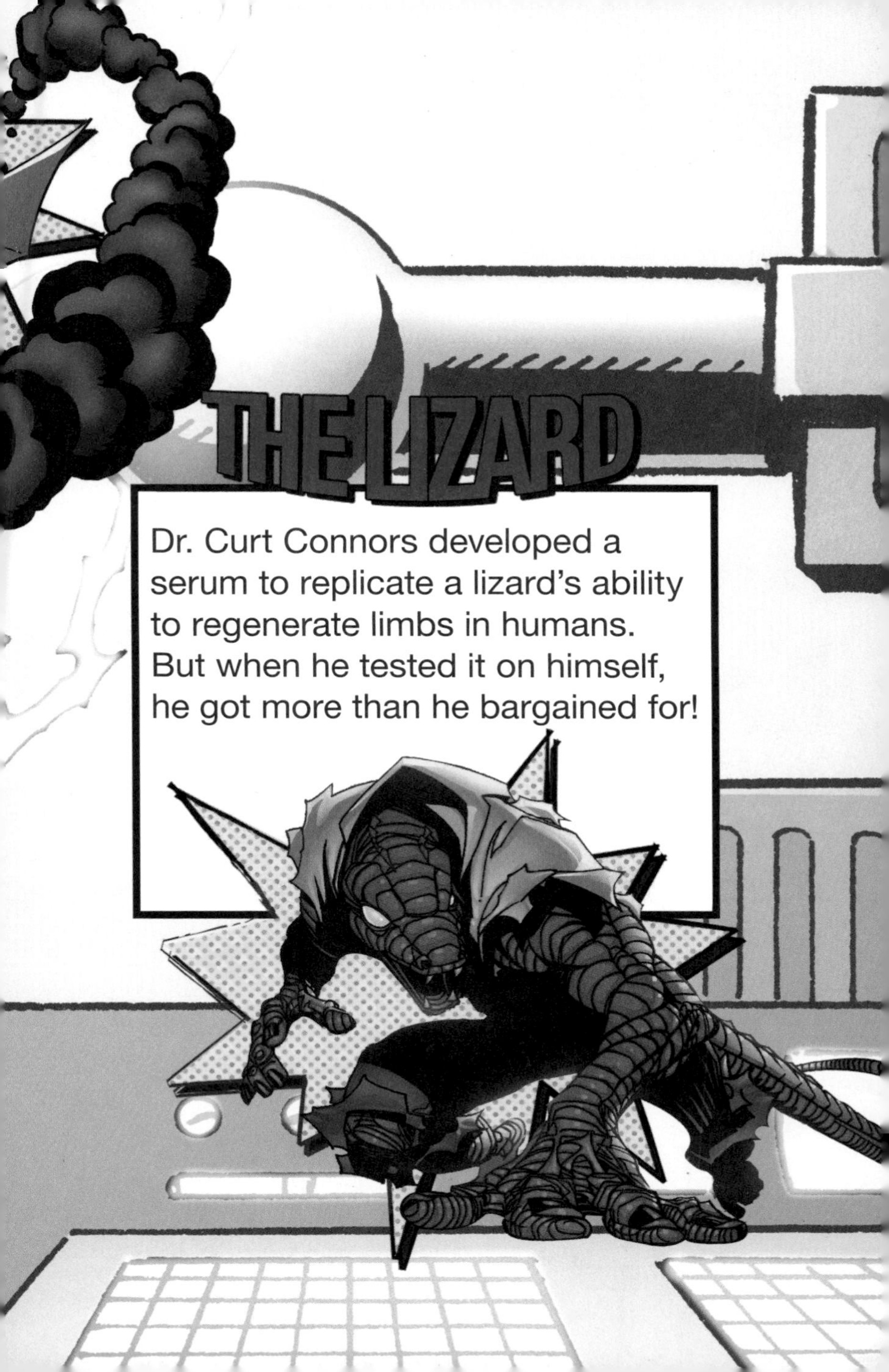
THE LIZARD
Dr. Curt Connors developed a serum to replicate a lizard's ability to regenerate limbs in humans. But when he tested it on himself, he got more than he bargained for!

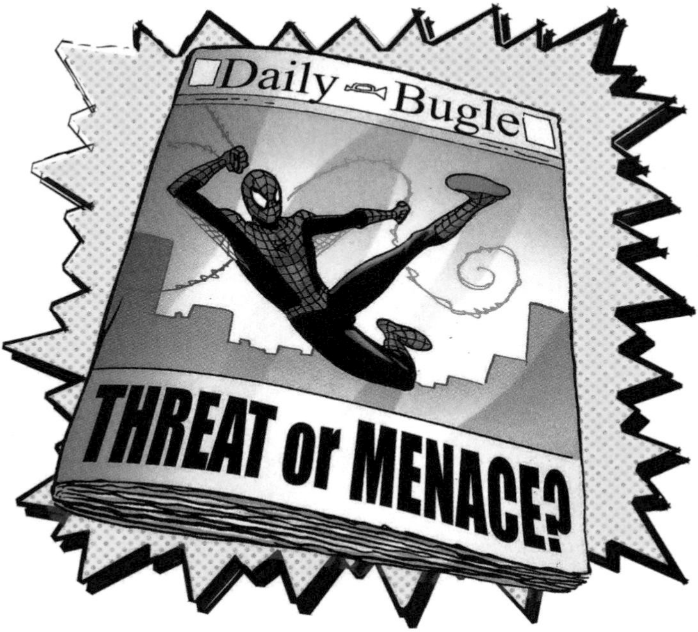
Daily Bugle
THREAT or MENACE?

CHAPTER
1

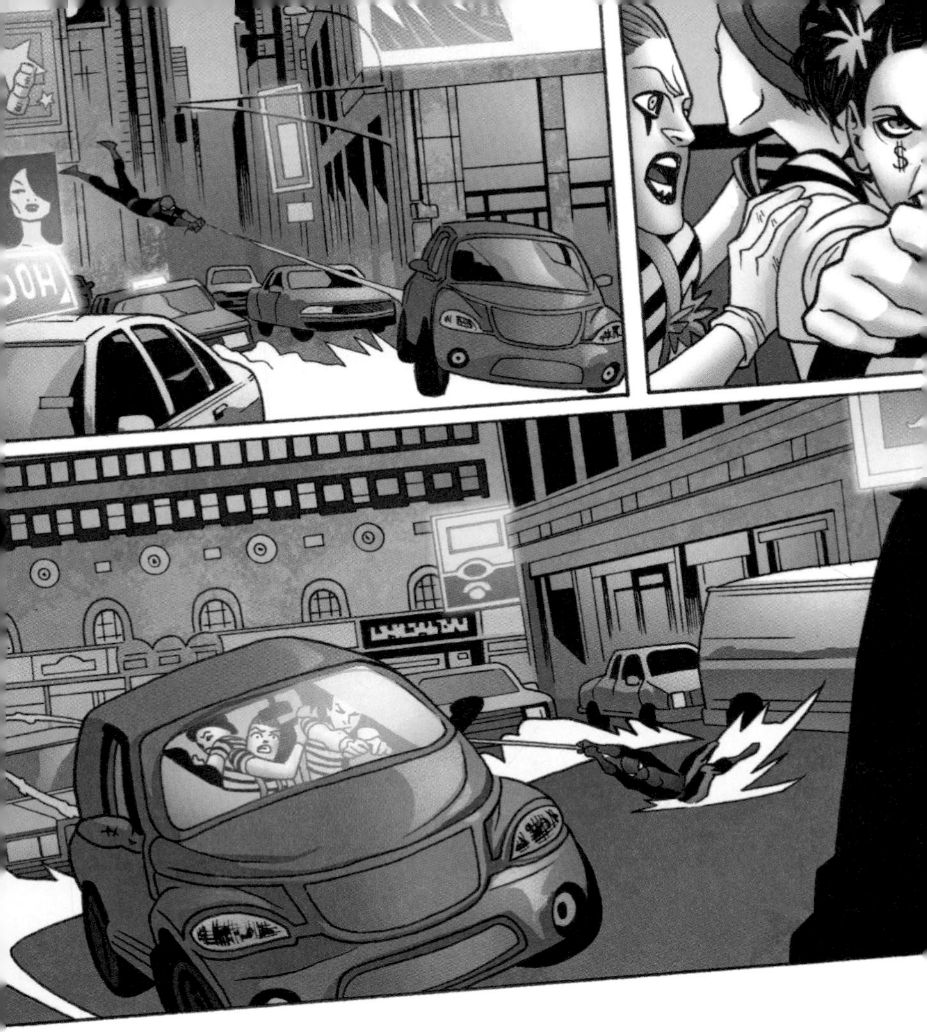

The tourists on their way to the Broadway matinees got a greater show than they bargained for that day! Theatergoers dove in all directions when the purple car skidded around the corner on two wheels before cutting into the midday traffic on 7th Avenue. Inside the car, three girls in French street mime costumes calling themselves Pinky, Binky and Sue shrieked loudly as the distant sound of police sirens drew closer.

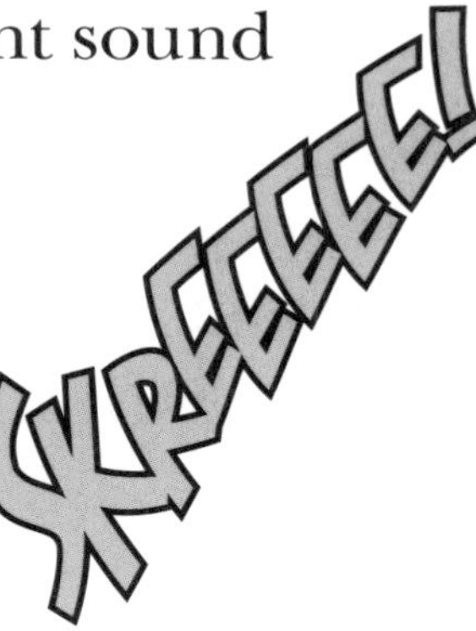
SKREEEEE!

Pinky pushed down on the gas pedal. As the car lurched forward, she checked the rear-view mirror to see if he was still there. "Are you sure that's him?" Binky asked. "Isn't he supposed to have, like, eight arms or something?"

"Who else could he be?" Pinky asked. "He's webbed to our bumper!" Sue looked out the rear windshield. Sure enough, he was *still* there: the skinny guy in the red-and-blue costume the newspapers were calling the Amazing Spider-Man!

But Spider-Man wasn't very happy to be there, either. It seemed like whenever there was a choice to be made, he seemed to make the wrong one. It all started a couple weeks ago when, while on a class trip, Peter Parker was bitten by a radioactive spider — and developed the proportional strength and abilities of the arachnid. But instead of using his new powers to do good deeds, he first used them to try to become rich and famous. Then one night when he had the chance to stop a burglar, he chose

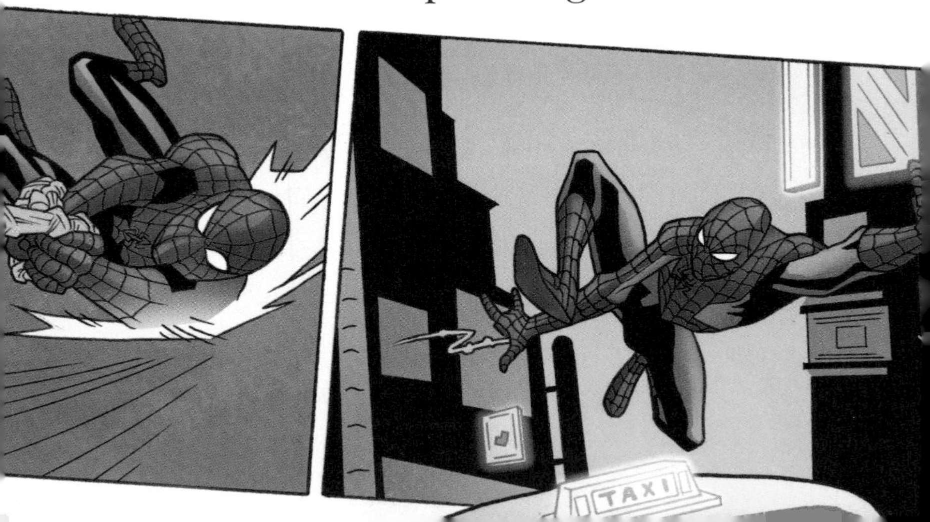
TAXI

to let him get away, instead. Later that
night, the same burglar broke into his
house and shot his Uncle Ben. Because
of his bad choices, he learned that
with great power, there must also come
great responsibility. Ever since, he's
been known as Spider-Man, New York
City's newest super-hero crime fighter!

When Pinky, Binky and Sue ran
from the bank with large bags of
money in their hands and got into
their getaway car, Spider-Man could
have stopped them
many different ways.
He chose what he
thought was the
easiest way and shot
a web to the bumper
of the car to keep it
from driving away.
Normally, that would
have worked, thanks

to his super-strength. But as the car zoomed away, Spider-Man was caught off-balance, yanked right off of his feet and dragged through midtown Manhattan!

As he was pulled across the asphalt, Spider-Man tried to get to his feet. *If I dig my heels in, I might be able to stand...like a water skier!* he thought. But when he sat up, he felt the rough city street chewing up the seat of his pants! If he wanted to keep his costume on (and in one piece) he had to come up with a better plan.

He let go of the web with one hand. As he zoomed through the next intersection, he aimed his wrist and pressed a small button in the palm of his hand. With a *THWIP!,* a web fired from the web-shooter bracelet hidden beneath his costume and stuck to the thick base of a passing lamppost!

With one web on the car and another on the lamppost, Spider-Man pulled them both with all his might. Searing pain shot all the way up to Spider-Man's shoulders. The spinning wheels of the purple car screeched as it veered across two lanes of traffic. It bounced up on the curb, across the sidewalk and right through the glass storefront of an Italian restaurant with a loud *SMASH!* It worked!

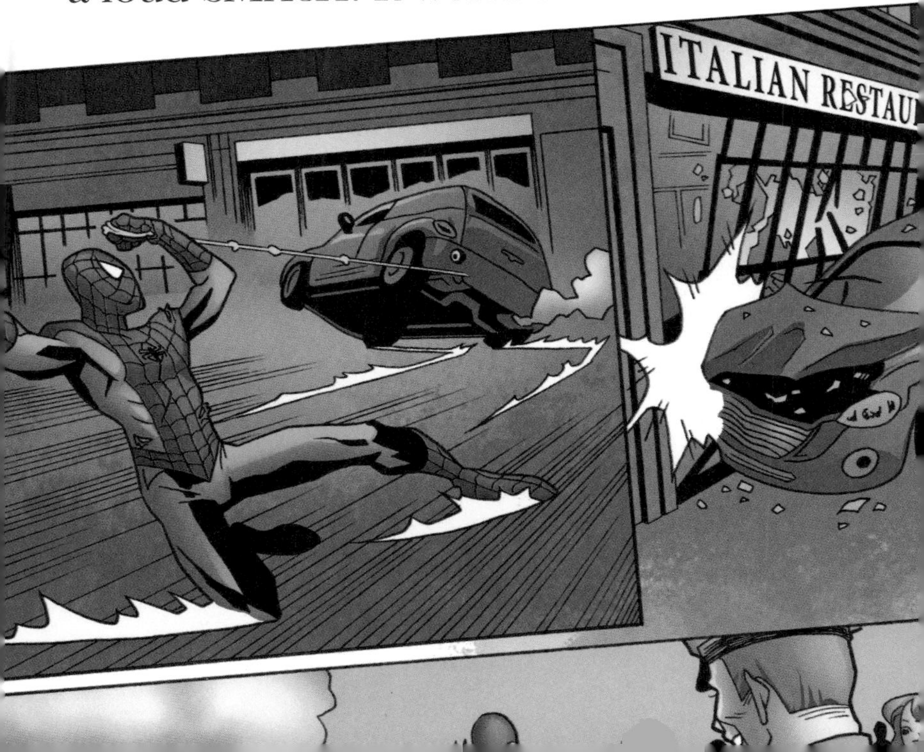
ITALIAN RESTAU

A police car with flashing red lights pulled up to the scene, and two officers jumped out to clear innocent bystanders out of the way. When they waved away the white smoke pouring out of the hood of the purple car, there were Pinky and Binky with their white mime faces planted firmly in the front-seat airbags. "I surrender!" shouted Sue from the backseat.

Spider-Man pulled himself up to his feet, dusted off the well-worn knees of his costume and walked over to the site of the crash. Everyone on the sidewalk stopped and stared. It was really *him!* Because he spent his days at Midtown High School as honors student Peter Parker (or "Pete the Science Geek," as the football team called him) he did most of his super-hero work at night. This was the first time Peter took the Spidey suit out for a spin in broad daylight. He walked down the street saluting and waving to the citizens of New York, the star of his own parade! But the crowd that should have been excited to see him instead whispered to each other and pointed at his back. One of the police officers noticed what they were seeing when he walked by and called out to him. "Hey, Spider-Man! Wait!"

"No need to thank me, officer," Spider-Man said. "It's just another day at the office for the Amazing Spider-Man!"

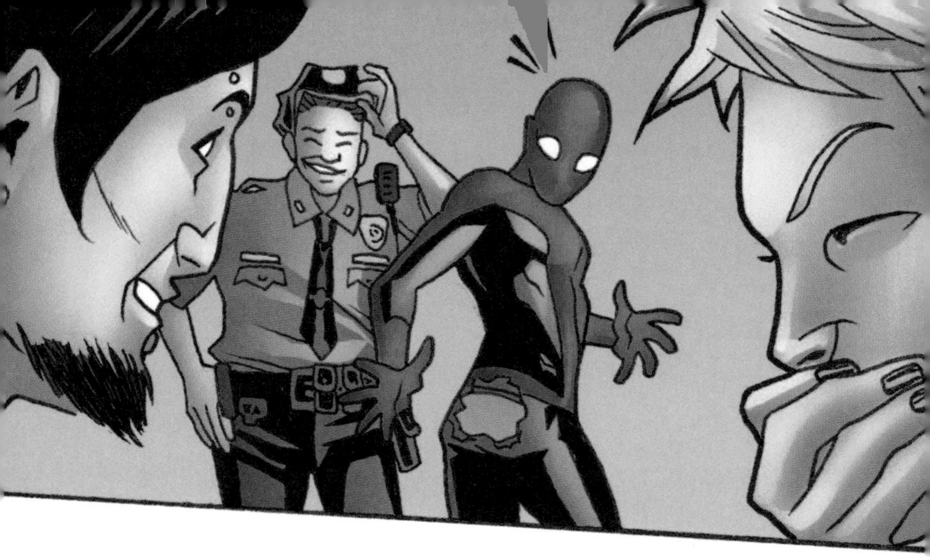

"No," the officer interrupted. "I mean..." Rather than finish his sentence, he politely twirled his finger to signal to the web-slinger to turn around. At first, Spider-Man didn't notice the giggling ladies snapping pictures behind him. But then he felt the breeze on his backside. The seat of his pants had been completely torn away, and his underpants were showing! The whole crowd roared with laughter! One by one, TV news vans and reporters

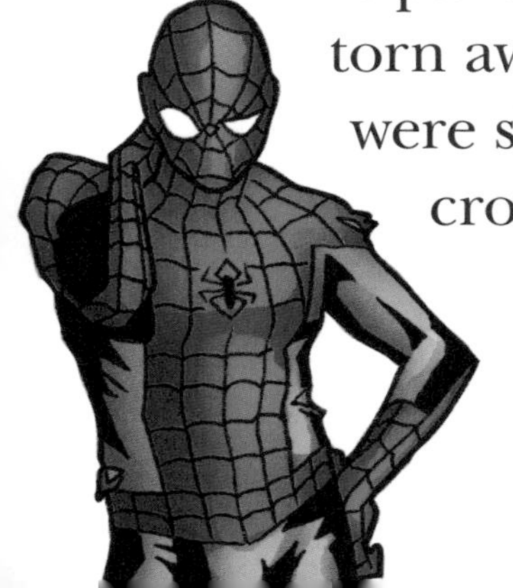

pulled up. Spider-Man knew that if he stuck around, his boxer shorts would be all over the six o'clock news. So with the push of a button on his web-shooter, he was out of sight in the blink of an eye. He was right: This *was* just another day for the Amazing Spider-Man — filled with bad luck.

The next morning, at the office of *The Daily Bugle* newspaper, its infamous Publisher J. Jonah Jameson slammed his fist down on a pile of that day's newspapers. *The New York Times, Daily News* and *New York Post* all had the biggest story of the year on their front pages: the news of Spider-Man's daytime debut right in the middle of Times Square!

"Every paper in the city is all over this," Jonah said. "Every newspaper except for the *Bugle!* And we wonder why our circulation is in the toilet!"

"Everyone's circulation is in the toilet," said *Bugle* Editor in Chief Joe "Robbie" Robertson as he stirred sugar into his coffee. Robbie was as cool as Jonah was fiery. He learned years ago that for *The Daily Bugle* to be a success, it needed him to be the voice of reason whenever J.J.J. flew off the handle, and today was no exception. "All the people we've got left were all downtown covering the Maggia trial," he said, taking a sip.

"Organized crime? That's *yesterday's* news, Robbie." Jonah jabbed a finger down on the newspapers. "Super heroes. Super villains. Weirdos with magical powers jumping around in their pajamas. Costumed vigilantes operating outside of the law. Now *there's* some news!"

"But before yesterday, nobody'd ever gotten a good look at him,"

Robbie replied.

"By the looks of these pictures, they still haven't. None of these pictures are showing anything but his goofy underpants!

"New plan, effective immediately: our top priority is to get any and all pictures of this Spider-Man, using *any* means necessary," said Jonah

"Uh-oh," Robbie leaned back in his chair, cupping his coffee mug between his hands. "I've seen that look. You're up to no good."

"If this Spider-Man wants to be famous," Jonah said, "we'll make him famous!"

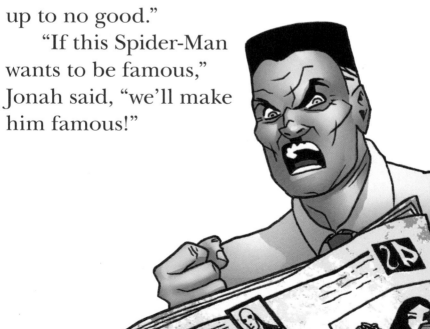

CHAPTER 2

The Marshall Corporation on the Upper East Side of Manhattan is where the future is being made. At least, that's what the sign outside says. The truth is, the company hasn't made anything but a mess since old Mr. Marshall retired and left his son, Albert, in charge.

Right from the start, Albert made steep budget cuts and moved most of the operations overseas. Those who were left in the New York factory were young, inexperienced and inexpensive. But the glue that held the company together was an old-timer named Adrian Toomes, who had been there so long he was practically furniture. Even though Mr. Toomes taught the young engineers everything he knew, they made fun of his bald head and old-fashioned ways behind his back. And once they became good at their jobs, the young engineers often left for better opportunities, leaving their old teacher behind.

On this day, the five o'clock bell signaled the end of the workday just as it had thousands of times before for Adrian Toomes, but this time it was different. Though Mr. Toomes didn't know it yet, it was the last time he would ever hear it. After he said

goodbye to the young engineers who were watching one of his demonstrations, he walked down the hall to his office to hang up his lab coat.

"Hello, Mr. Toomes." Albert Marshall had been waiting for him inside, which was never a good sign. Albert didn't exactly have a reputation for dropping by to give *good* news. "Nice bird," he said, admiring the green parrot that stood on a perch in the corner. Mr. Toomes was always interested in birds; he thought a bird in flight was Mother Nature's finest work of engineering. In fact, his office was decorated with bird pictures, statues and, for many years, his pet parrot, Menlo.

"What do you want, Albert?"

"Fine, Mr. Toomes, I'll just get right to it," Albert said as he paced back and forth, picking the lint off of his fancy Italian suit. "You've been with the Marshall Corp. for, what, ten...twelve years?"

"Thirty-six," Mr. Toomes said.

"Right," Albert said, not really caring. "Well, then you also know that for the past couple of years, business has been...less than great. So I've decided to make some changes — for example, maybe replace some of our old equipment with some newer, younger models."

Mr. Toomes was relieved. For a minute there, he thought he was getting fired.

"And that includes employees," Albert finished.

Mr. Toomes' face dropped. "Wait," he said. "You're FIRING ME?!"

"SQUAWWWWK!" Menlo wailed,

startling Albert so badly he nearly jumped right out of his shiny alligator shoes! He ducked down behind a chair.

“Mr. Toomes, this company was founded on cutting-edge technology.

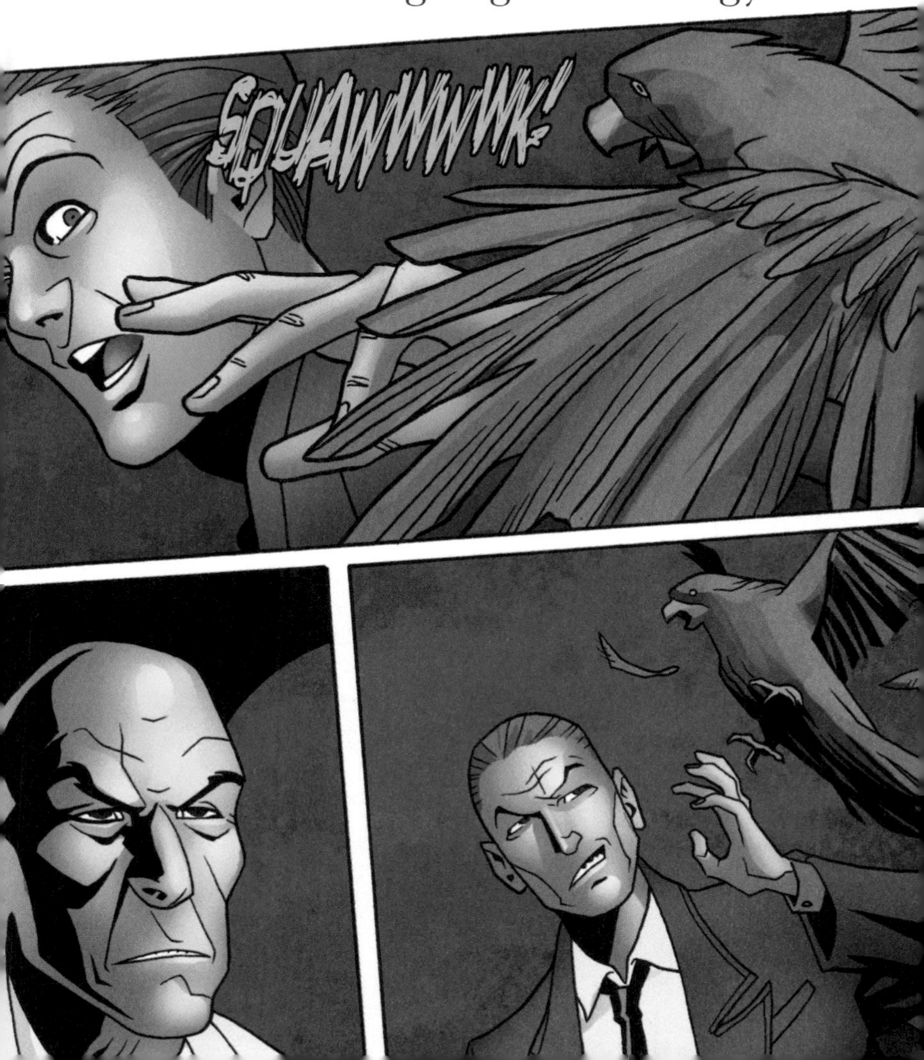
SQUAWWWWK!

Today, the competition is fierce. And you...you haven't brought a worthwhile pitch to the floor since you had a full head of hair."

"But what about the Vulture?"

"The Vulture?" Albert asked, slowly standing up now that Menlo had calmed down. "You mean your...bird suit?"

"It's not a *bird suit*. The Vulture is a harness that turns an average human being into a low-cost, eco-friendly aerial-assault weapon. The Department of Defense might have use for something like that."

Albert swallowed hard to hold down his laughter. "A harness?"

Mr. Toomes flipped open his appointment book. "If you want, I can schedule a demonstration —"

"I'm sorry, Mr. Toomes," he interrupted, "but it has already been

decided. You have one hour to pack
up your things. Security will escort you
out of the building" And with that, he
walked to the door.

"Albert, wait!" Mr. Toomes put his
face down in his hands. "My retirement
account was wiped out in the stock-
market crash. This job is all I have.
*Please.*"

"You know, Dad always said you
were the most resourceful man he

knew," Albert said. "I'm sure you'll think of something." Menlo the parrot flew off of his perch in a rage, pecking and flapping his wings against Albert's head! "SQUAWWWWK!" Albert covered his head and ran screaming down the hall!

"Let him go, Menlo," Mr. Toomes said. "It's *my* fault. All my life, I've let people like him walk all over me. But *never again!* I'm too old for that now.

"Albert's right, I *am* resourceful... and I know exactly what I have to do. And finally everyone will know that the *Vulture* is no laughing matter!"

Peter Parker zigzagged along the sidewalk, sidestepping children, briefcases and umbrella handles

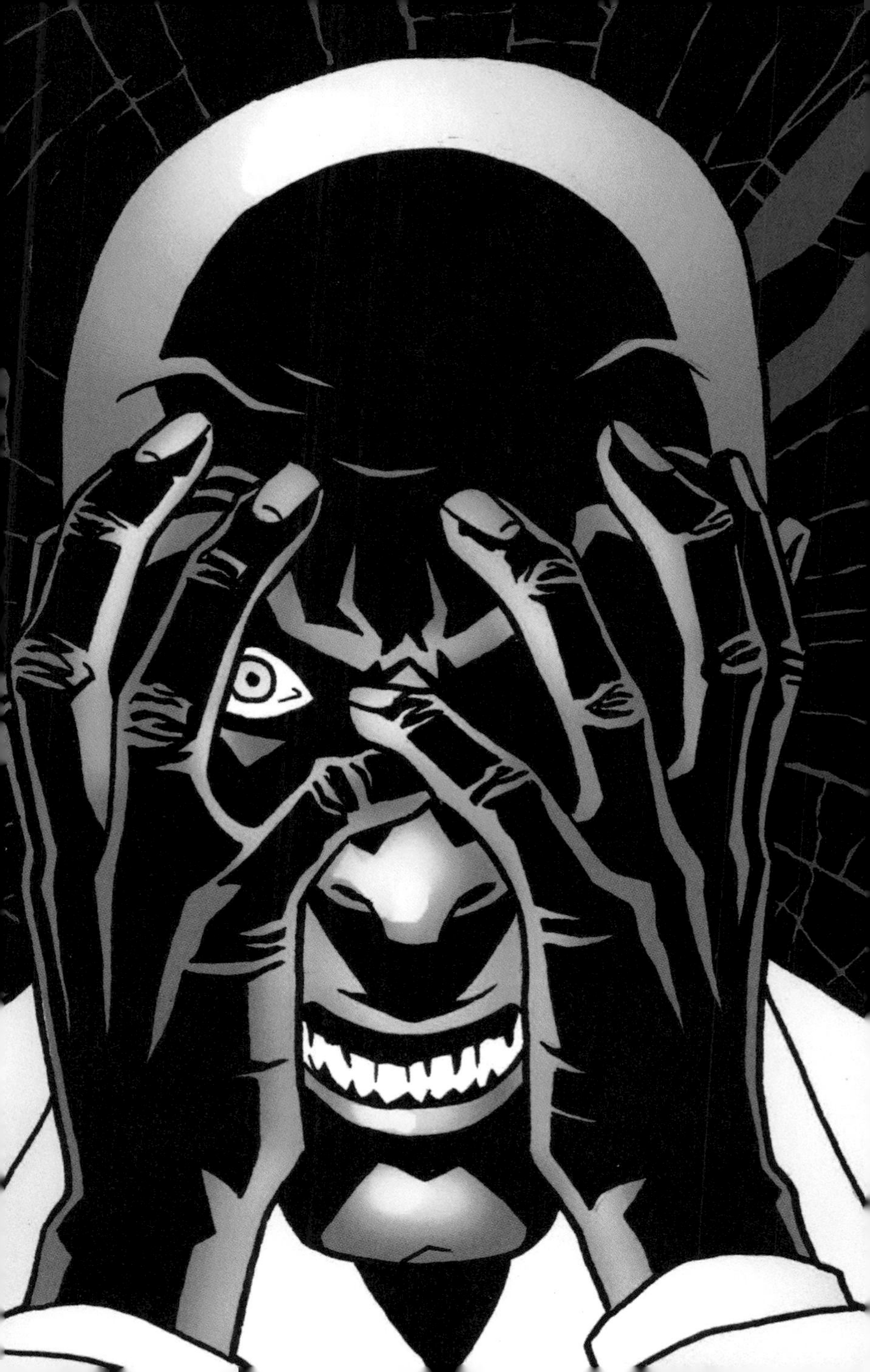

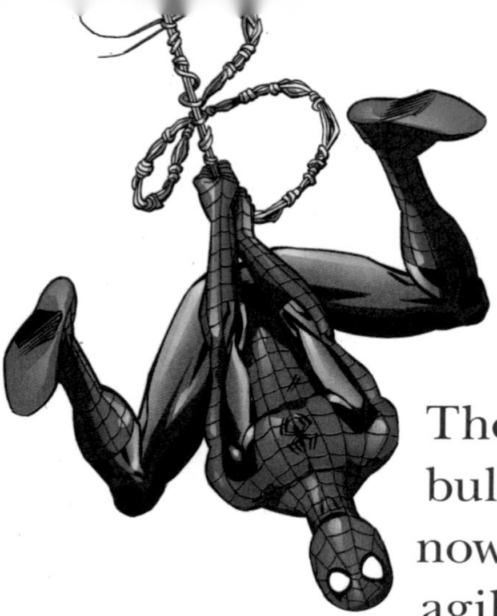

with ease. In the past, he'd have a hard time getting away from Flash Thompson and his bully buddies. But now that he had super-agility, it was all too easy. If he wanted, he could take on all of them with his super-strength and be sure they'd never bother him again, but he had to be very careful to keep his powers hidden so nobody would find out he was really Spider-Man. It was best to avoid confrontation completely.

The signal at the crosswalk said "Don't Walk." But with Flash and his buddies gaining on him, Peter took a deep breath and crossed the busy street, anyway. Flash was going to follow, but thought better of it when he got to the curb. *Nobody in his right mind would ever run into that rush-hour traffic,* he thought. *Is Parker crazy?* Then again, nobody had Peter Parker's super-agility either. He was home free! "You can't run forever, Puny Parker!" Flash shouted.

Peter laughed as he closed the door to his building behind him, but his good mood didn't last very long when he saw the eviction notice taped to Aunt May's apartment door. He

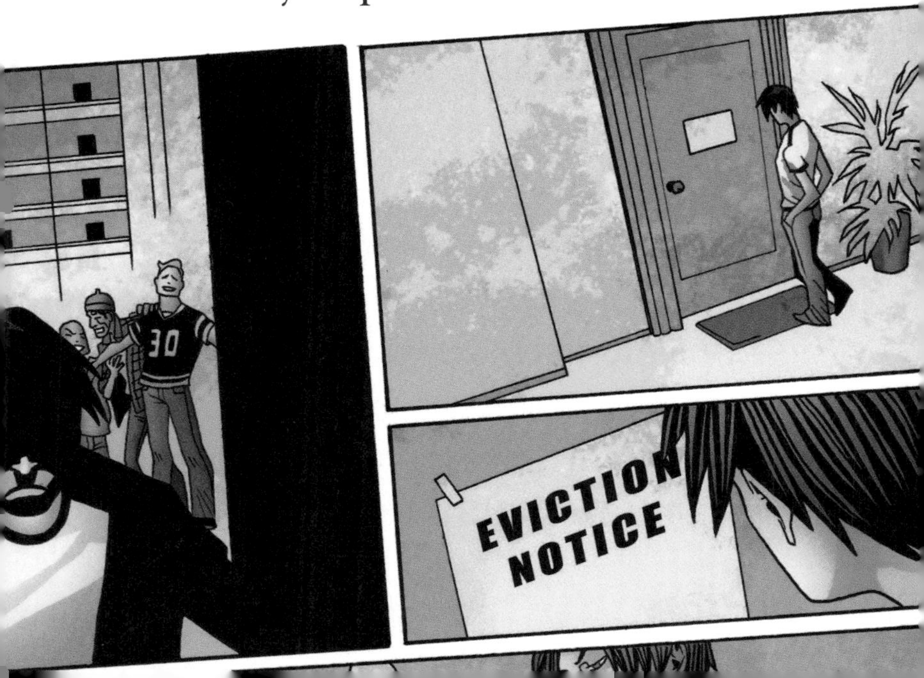
30
EVICTION
NOTICE

knew Aunt May was going to have trouble paying the rent after Uncle Ben passed away, but he didn't realize how bad things already were. He never expected they might be thrown out of their home.

Peter ripped the notice from the door and crumpled it in his hand. Aunt May heard him come in and peeked out from the kitchen to greet him. She was her usual cheerful self, but now Peter wondered whether it was all just an act. What else had she been hiding from him?

"Peter?" she asked. But he didn't respond. Instead, he headed straight up the stairs to his room without a word.

"Peter, wait!" she said, catching up to him on the stairs. "Before you go up and disappear into your room, there's something important I need to tell you."

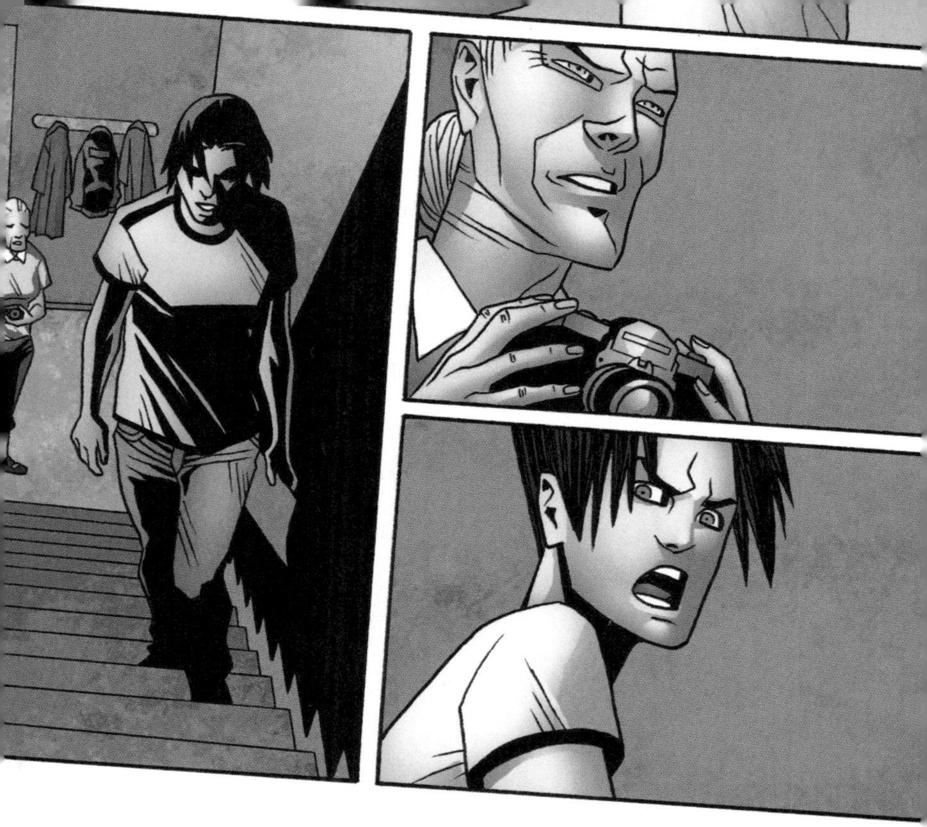

Peter held up his fist that had the crumpled-up eviction notice in it. "I already saw it," he said, and then started back up the stairs.

"No, not that," she said, stopping him again. Then she held up a camera. "*This.* Our neighbor Willie Lumpkin thinks it might be worth something. It's an antique, but it has a self-timer. I found it in a box of things from Uncle Ben's closet and —"

"WHAT?!" Peter shouted. He couldn't believe it! Uncle Ben had just passed away, and Aunt May was already selling his stuff! "Put it back! PUT IT *ALL* BACK!"

"Peter." Aunt May approached him gently. "I know you feel a lot of guilt over the way things ended with Uncle Ben. I do, too! I know what you're going through."

But she *didn't* know. She knew Peter and Uncle Ben had an argument before he died, but she didn't know Peter felt personally responsible for what happened to his uncle. "No, you don't. You can't!"

"Well, then tell me! Instead of staying out all day and locking yourself in your room all night, tell me so I can understand!"

“I —” Peter replied. “Just please don’t sell his stuff!”

“But you didn’t let me finish! In that same box, I found *this*.” She held up a little brown leather notebook. “It’s a bankbook from one of Uncle Ben’s old accounts. I called the bank...and it’s still active.

“Peter, we have the rent money!”

Peter couldn’t hold back any

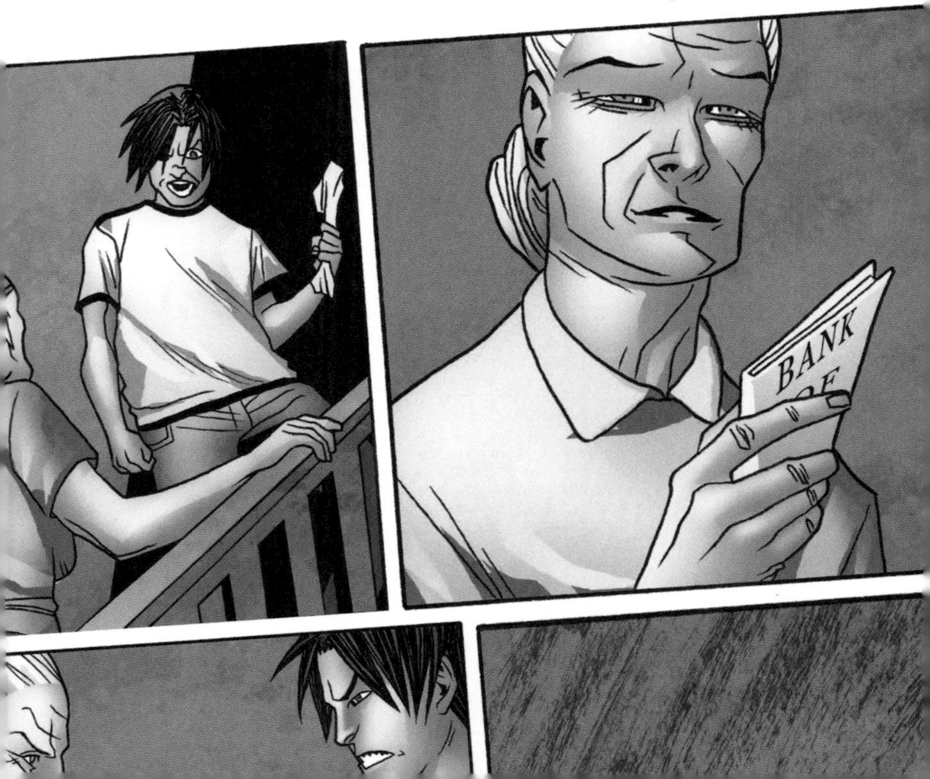
BANK

longer. At once, all of those tears he'd been holding in for so many days came pouring down his face. Aunt May hugged him tight around the neck.

"There, there," she said. "Everything's going to be all right from now on. I promise."

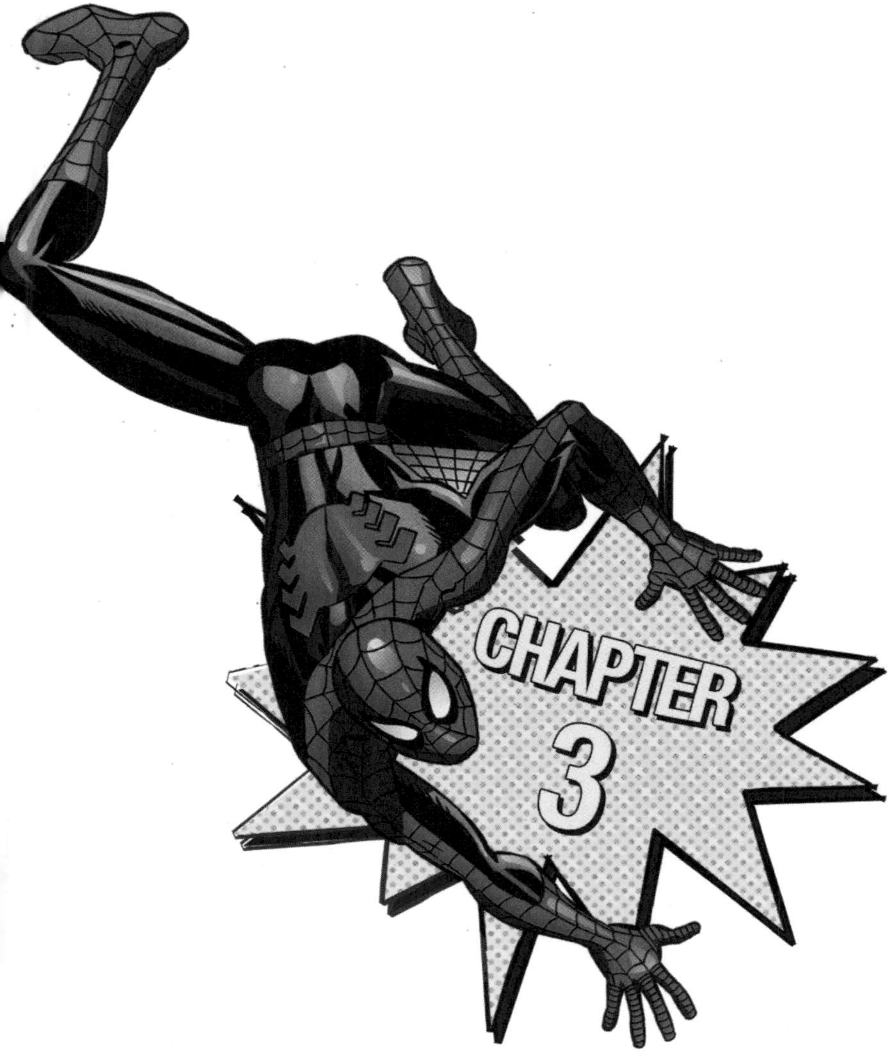
CHAPTER
3

The Greater Community Bank of New York City's lobby was so big the sound of the woman's tapping at her computer keyboard echoed high into the vaulted ceiling and fell down like rain all around Aunt May and Peter as they sat patiently in their seats. The sunlight coming in through the high glass walls shone on them brightly like a spotlight. Peter had brought Uncle Ben's old camera with him, and he

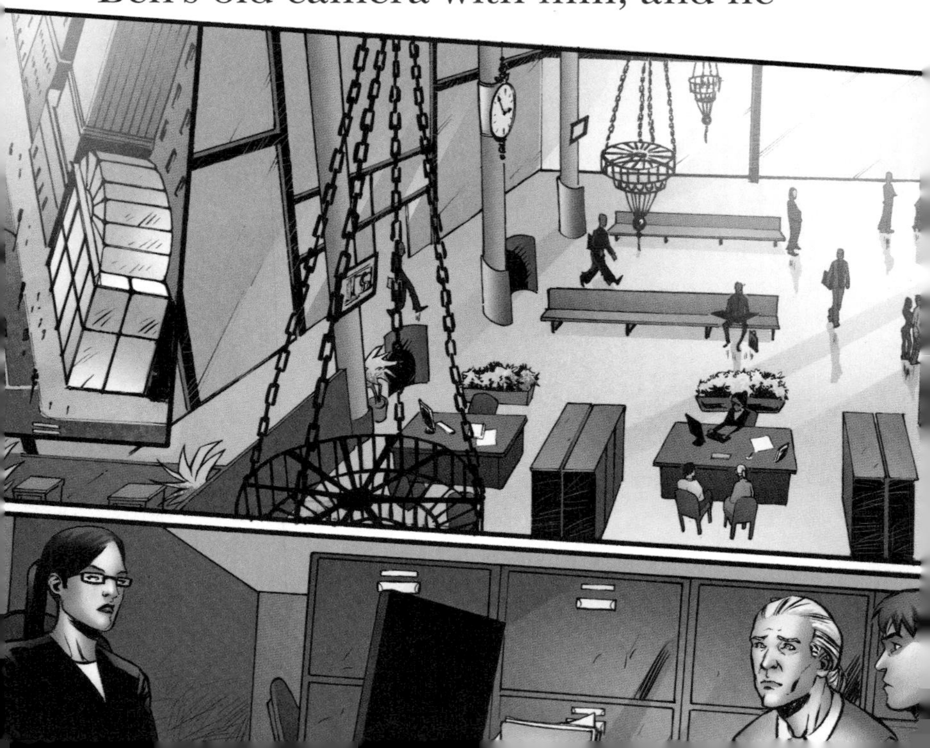

fiddled with it nervously. When they were finished, he wanted to take some photos around the city and bring the film to the old camera store in their neighborhood to be developed and turned into a scrapbook. On the subway ride to the bank, Aunt May told Peter that years ago when Uncle Ben was in college, he had his own darkroom where he used a chemical solution and photo paper to develop his film into photographs. She said Peter could turn the upstairs bathroom into his own darkroom if he wanted to experiment. Aunt May knew Peter loved science and would never be able to resist such a project!

Between rounds of frantic typing that seemed to go on forever, the bank lady, Miss Maloney, glared at them over her glasses — and then pushed her

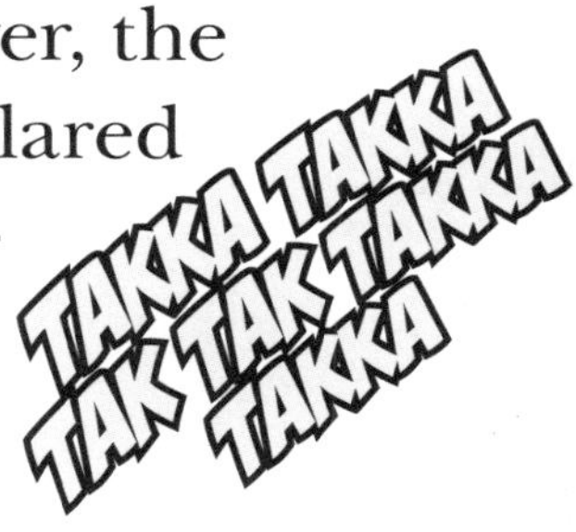
TAKKA TAKKA
TAK TAK TAKKA
TAKKA

glasses up the bridge of her nose and tapped at the keys again.

"Is there a problem?" Aunt May finally asked.

"Your husband didn't add you to this account, Mrs. Parker?"

"He's had it since before we were married..."

Miss Maloney returned to her typing, and then glared at Aunt May over her glasses again. "It wasn't in his will?" she asked.

"It isn't much without all of the interest added in," Aunt May replied. "It must have slipped his mind."

Miss Maloney removed her glasses and smiled. *Finally! A good sign!* Aunt May thought as she squeezed Peter's hand.

"I'm sorry, Mrs. Parker," Miss Maloney said. "There's nothing I can do for you."

Aunt May sprang from her chair. "What?" Peter gently squeezed her hand to get her to sit back down again. "I mean...there must be a way to..."

Miss Maloney leaned forward and crossed her hands on her desk like a stern schoolteacher. "Mrs. Parker, bank policy states we'd need a signed and notarized letter from the account holder before letting you withdraw the funds."

This time, it was Peter who leapt from his chair. "That'd be kind of hard to get *now*, don't you think?!"

"Peter, please!" Aunt May grabbed his arm and pulled him back down. "Just go back to playing with your camera."

Peter couldn't believe Aunt May had dismissed him like that. He was the man of the house now. And a super hero, to boot! He could do whatever a spider could and spin a web of any size to catch thieves like flies! *If Aunt May only knew,* he thought.

"Excuse me, Miss Maloney, but may I speak with a manager, please?" Aunt May asked calmly.

"Mrs. Parker, I don't see how that will make any difference."

Aunt May started to lose her patience. "This is very urgent, so can you PLEASE GET ME A MANAGER?!" Miss Maloney scurried off to find one without further argument.

While they waited, Peter loaded a roll of film into the old camera and put it up to his eye. The zoom lens was out of focus, so he aimed at a faraway rooftop through the glass walls and noticed an odd, green figure. He slowly turned the lens to focus and saw it was an old man. An old man in a peculiar green costume with large wings! And with the old man's beak-like nose and bald head, he kind of looked like a bird.

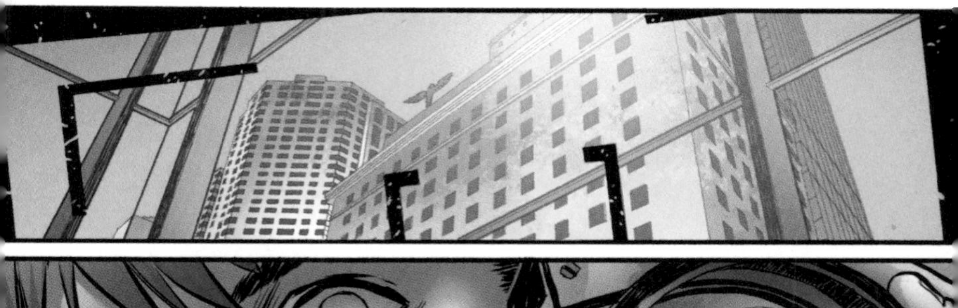

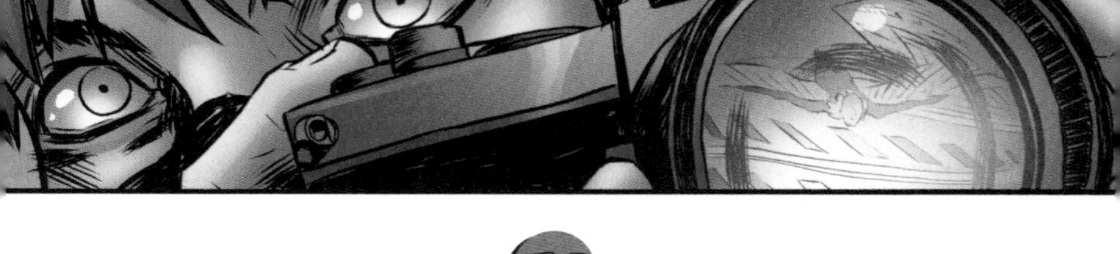

Before Peter could show him to Aunt May, the man took a running start and jumped off the roof! Peter put the camera down to see with his own eyes. There was the man, gliding across the busy street on those magnificent wings...headed right for the bank!

When the Vulture crashed through the glass, shattering half the wall to pieces, Peter pulled Aunt May down to the floor behind the desk to cover her. Customers ran for the front door. Bank tellers ducked behind the counter. The security guard closest to the intruder reached for his gun, but the Vulture grabbed him by the throat and lifted him high in the air

before he could unholster it. He spun the guard around and threw him into another security guard who was sneaking over to help. By the time

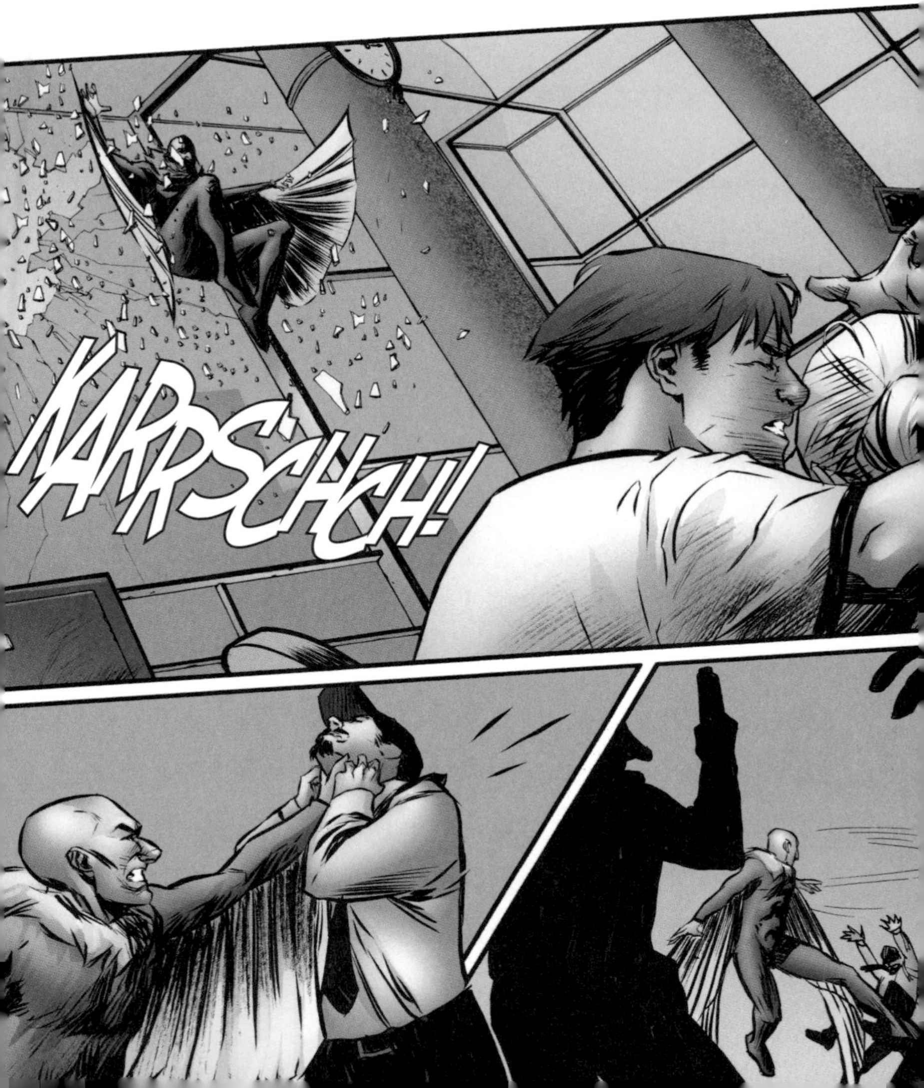
KARRSCHCH!

the Vulture noticed the third security guard, his gun was already drawn. The guard fired three shots! But the Vulture shielded himself with one of his wings, and the bullets bounced off harmlessly. They were bulletproof! Then, the Vulture thrust his arm toward the guard. Several razor-sharp feathers launched from the wing, hitting their target with precision.

"A-all right," the Vulture said. "Everyone stay calm. I don't want to hurt anyone. Just stay where you are, and everything will be fine."

After he made sure Aunt May was

all right, Peter told her to stay put and began to crawl away from their hiding place. "Peter, where are you going?" she whispered loudly, grabbing him by the shirt.

"I'm just...going to get some pictures." But what Peter really had in mind was to find a place to stash Uncle Ben's old camera and change into the

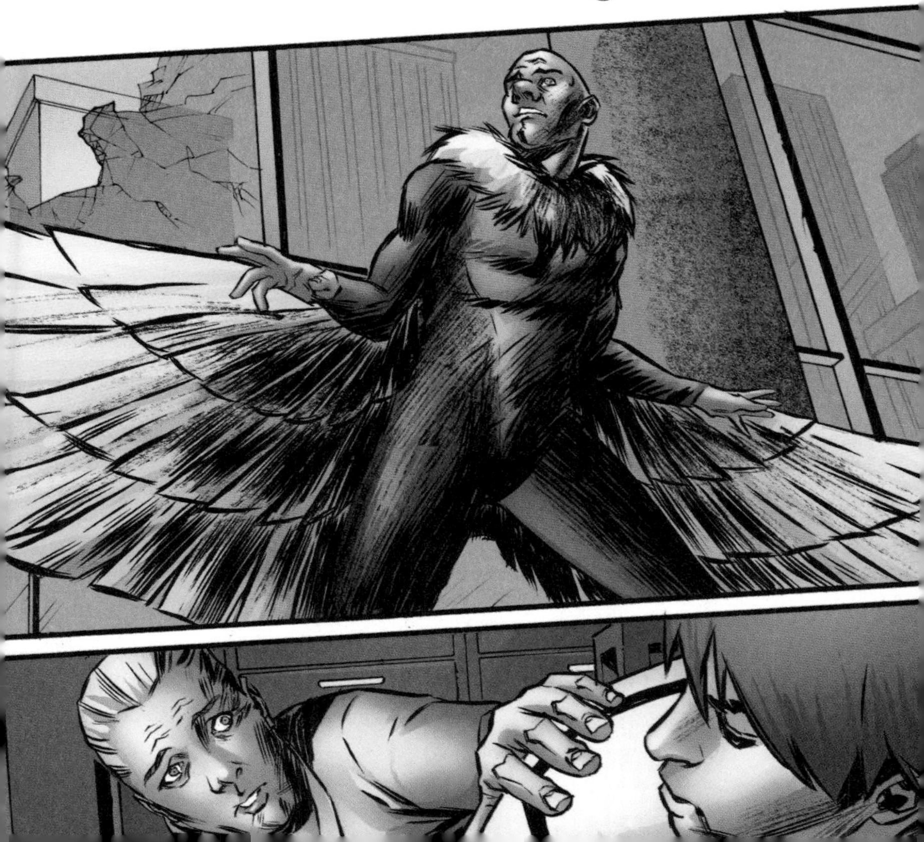

red-and-blue Spider-Man costume he
had begun wearing under his clothes
in case of emergencies like this one.
Aunt May tried to stop him, but he
disappeared into the maze of desks too
quickly.

"Peter, no!"

"You!" The Vulture grabbed Miss
Maloney by the shoulders and shook
her. "Get a trash bag, and lead me to
the vault!"

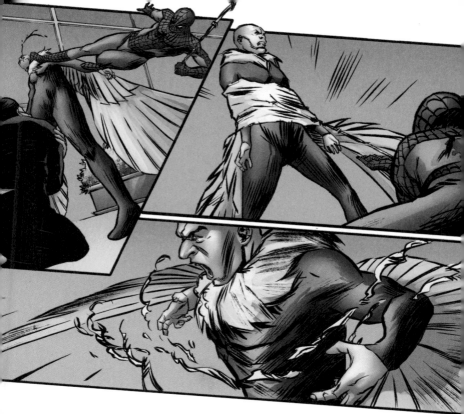

Then, as quick as a flash, Spider-Man swung across the room and kicked the Vulture in the side of the head, knocking him off of his feet. Miss Maloney landed hard on the floor, but crawled safely into the corner. "I don't believe my eyes!" Spider-Man said. "Just when I thought it couldn't get any weirder than a

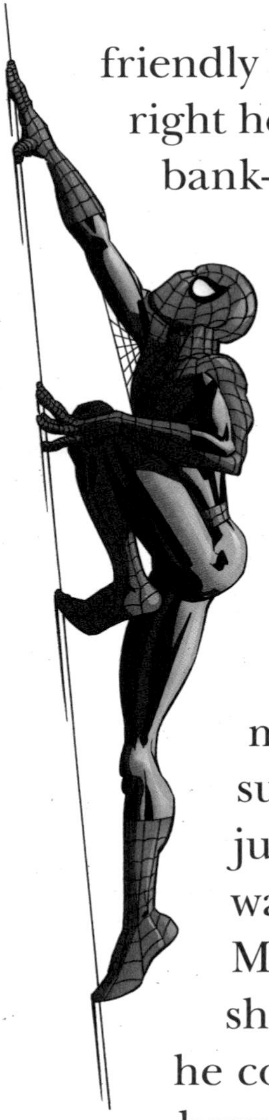

friendly neighborhood Spider-Man, right here, as I live and breathe, is a bank-robbing *buzzard*!"

"The Spider-Man?"

This was more than the Vulture had expected on his first outing as a super villain. Spider-Man aimed both web-shooters at him and sprayed webs around his body, wrapping him up around the ribs like a mummy. But in the Vulture suit, Adrian Toomes wasn't just an ordinary old man; he was a lot stronger than Spider-Man knew. He popped his sharp wings out as hard as he could against the webs that bound him, and they sliced through the sticky webbing with ease. He was free!

"This is not what I wanted!" the Vulture said. He jumped up, flapped his wings. Before anyone knew it, he was flying higher and higher toward the ceiling. Spider-Man wasn't about to let another criminal get away the way he did the night of Uncle Ben's murder and shot a web at his legs to slow him down.

"Hey, it's not what I wanted either, Buzzy, but we don't have much of a choice now." But instead of Spider-Man's web pulling the Vulture down,

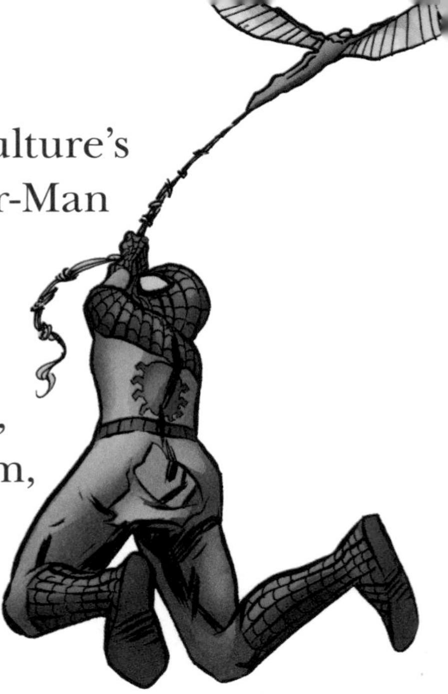

the power of the Vulture's wings pulled Spider-Man up! And up and up and up they went!

Then, once Miss Maloney saw it, she called out to him, "Hey, Spider-Man?"

But he didn't need to hear the rest of what she was going to say. He knew as soon as he felt the breeze on his backside. *Crud,* he thought to himself, *I didn't get a chance to fix my pants.*

CHAPTER
4

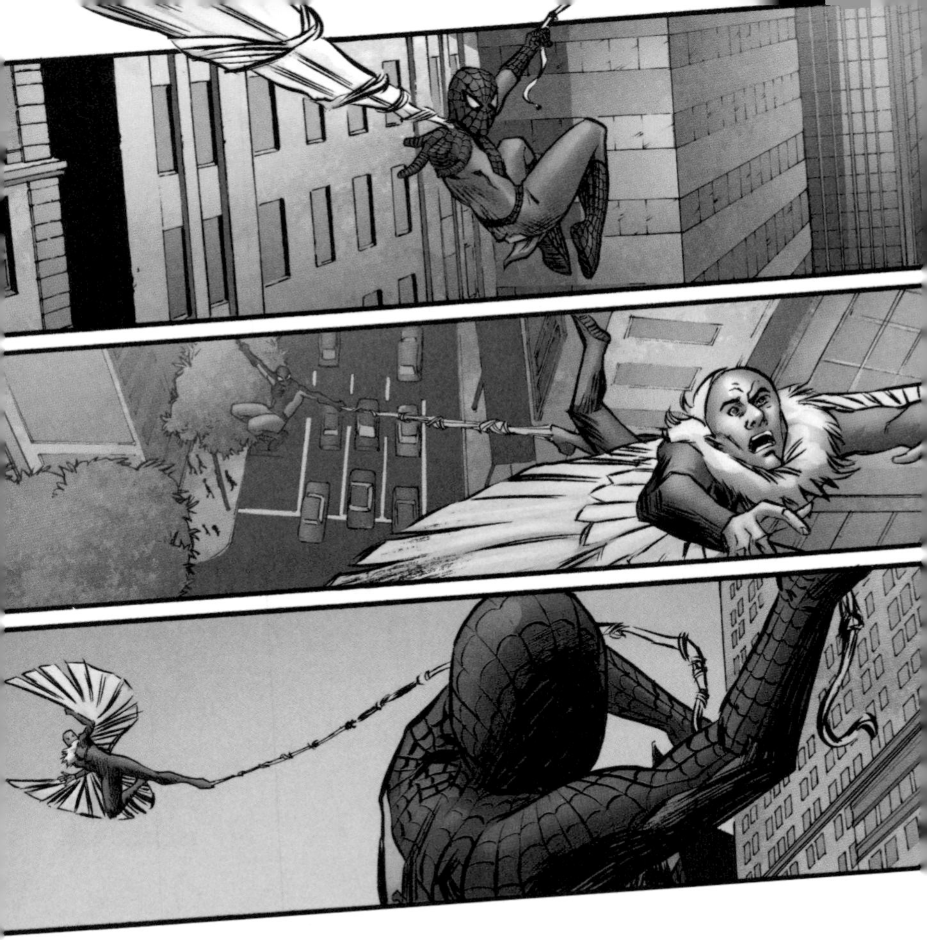

The Vulture pulled Spider-Man so high they crashed right through the glass ceiling of the Greater Community Bank...and kept on going! But no matter how high they flew, Spider-Man still held on! The Vulture weaved in between buildings, turned sharply around corners, but Spider-Man still held on! He twisted and twirled in the air, climbed and fell sharply, but Spider-Man *still* held on! He used every trick his Vulture suit was capable of, but he just couldn't get Spider-Man off his tail!

Holding on to the web for dear life, Spider-Man he had made the wrong choice again. He had no real plan for how to stop the Vulture aside from holding on to that web with all of his might! It was just like when he was dragged by Pinky, Binky and Sue's purple car. *That's it!* he thought, *I know what I have to do!* While holding on to his web with one hand, he reached out with his other

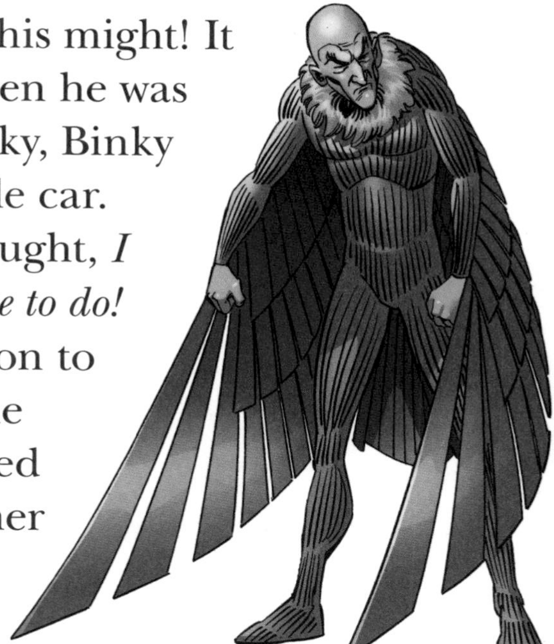

and fired a web at a nearby building. It stuck! And with a web held firmly in each hand — one attached to the building and the other to the Vulture's leg — he pulled Toomes to an abrupt stop in mid-air!

Then, Spider-Man yanked the Vulture back to him, and they grappled in the air as they tumbled toward the streets below! "Nice outfit," Spider-Man said. "Is today your day off from greeting customers outside of Frank's Chicken Hut, grandpa?"

"You underestimate me, spider-boy!" Toomes replied. "The Vulture harness doesn't just give me the ability to fly, it gives me the strength of twenty men!"

Though the Vulture had a good grip on him, Spider-Man was able to wrestle his arm free. "Congratulations. But

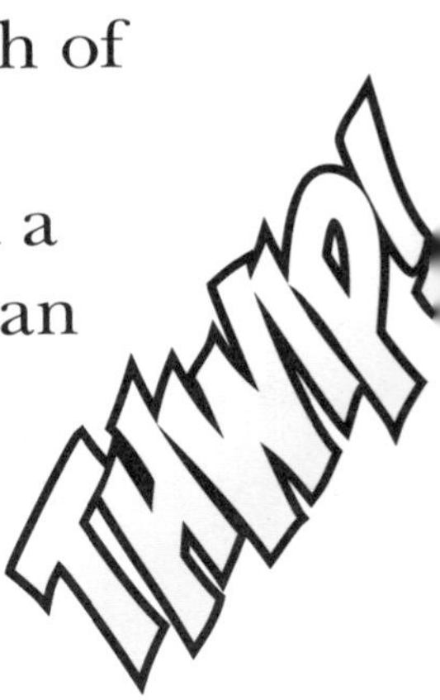
THWIP!

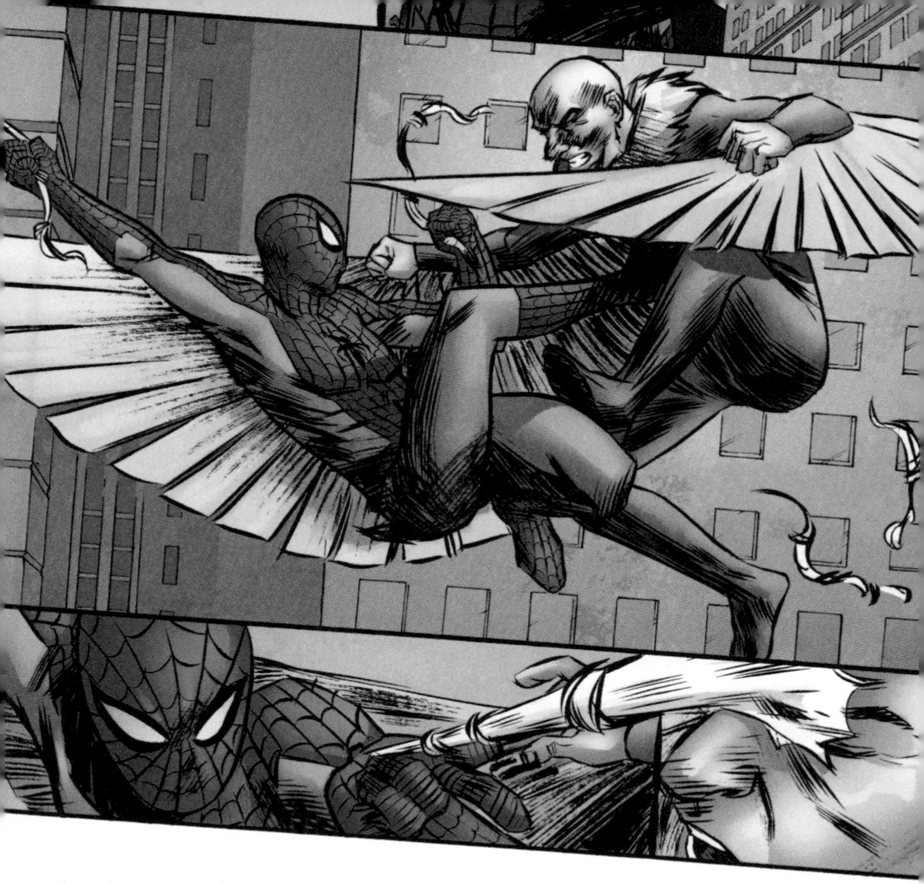

let's see how you do FLYING BLIND!" With the push of a button, the web-shooter shot a sticky blob of webbing right across the Vulture's eyes, covering them like a mask.

The Vulture grabbed at his face, trying to peel it off. Without his sight, he was no match for anyone! He tried to fly away, but this time Spider-Man learned from his mistake. With a hard tug on the web, he vaulted himself right onto the Vulture's back!

"You're not good at this at all," Spider-Man said. "Maybe you'd better let *me* steer for a while."

He held the webs like reins, pulling the Vulture this way and that. The Vulture tried to wriggle free, but couldn't. While they fought over

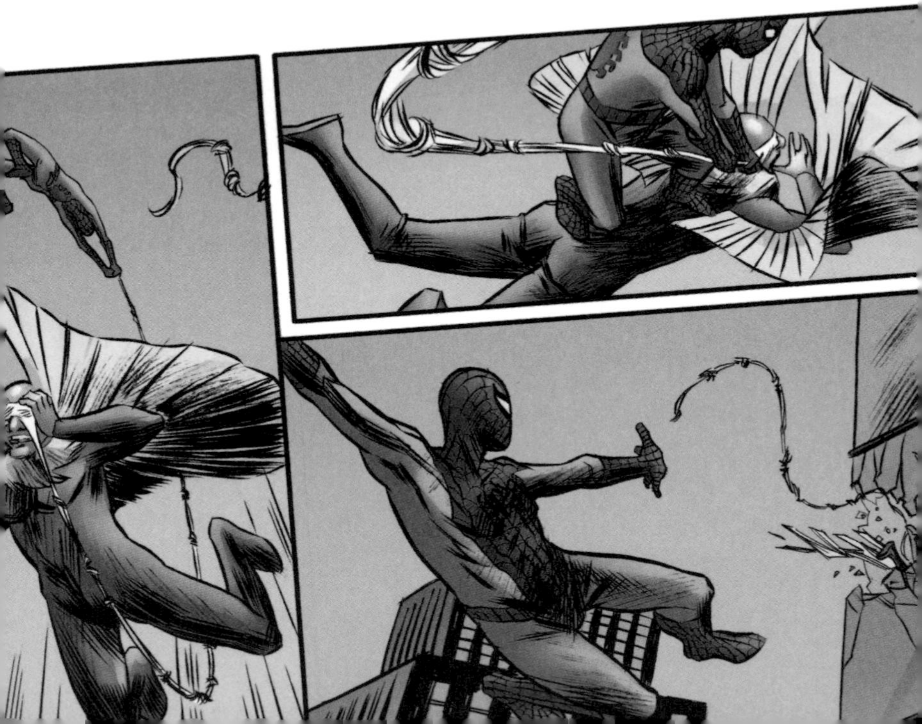

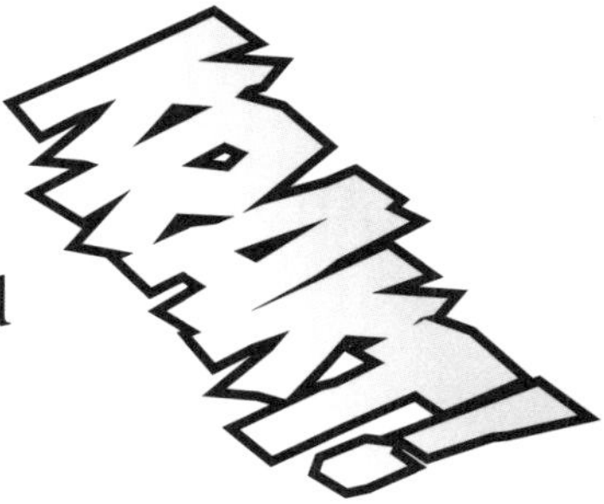

control, they suddenly realized they were headed straight for a skyscraper.

"Let go!" the Vulture screamed. "You'll kill us both!"

"Okay, have it your way!" When Spider-Man let go of the reins, he gave the Vulture one last shove to send him crashing through a window! He crawled through the window to make sure Toomes didn't get away, and found the injured old man lying in a pile of broken glass and furniture. The harness may have given him extraordinary abilities, but Adrian Toomes was still just a man in a bird suit who was in way over his head. "Serves you right for flying without a license," Spider-Man quipped as he carefully webbed up his foe's arms and wings tightly so there'd be no escape this time. Spider-Man carried him from out of the wreckage and gently lowered him to the ground, where two police officers were waiting to take him away.

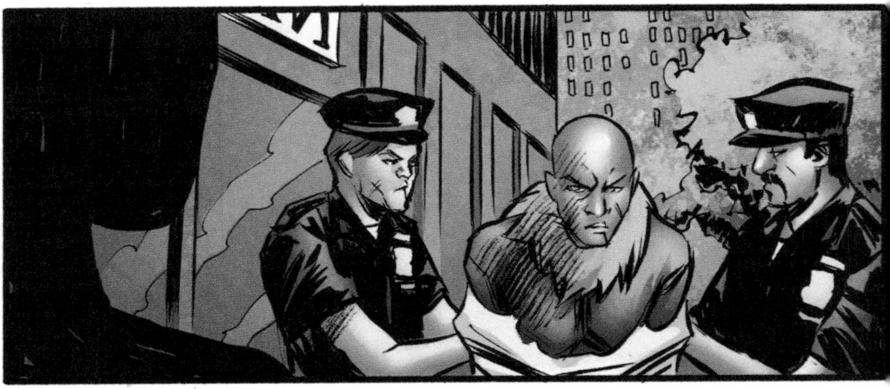

"You're just a kid," Toomes said as the police officers closed the handcuffs around his wrists. "You don't know what it's like to be all alone. To be out of money. I had no choice."

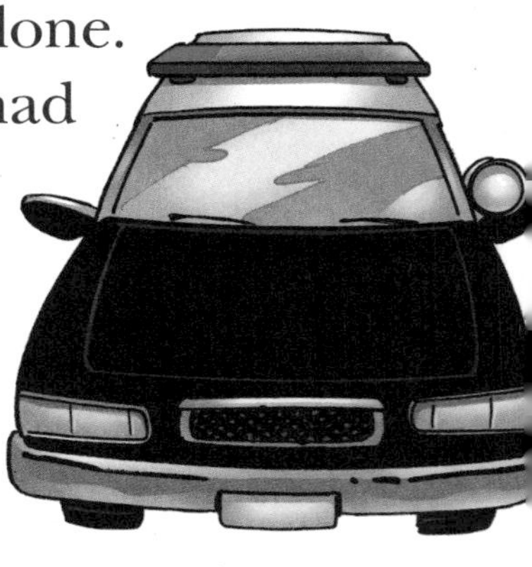

"That's where you're wrong," Spider-Man said. As Peter

Parker, he and Aunt
May were about to
get kicked out of
their apartment
because they
didn't have rent
money. "We
can't always control the things
that happen to us, but how we react
to them is always our choice." The
policemen tipped their caps to Spider-
Man and led the Vulture to their
squad car.

"I CAN'T BELIEVE IT!" A man
shouted from behind.

"I know, I know," Spidey answered.
"I didn't get a chance to fix my pants."

"It's you! Spider-Man! Right
here in front of me! And this stupid
battery's dead on my camera! I could
have finally paid off my student loans!
Stupid! Stupid! Stupid!"

Spider-Man saw the man with a goatee and baseball cap shaking his camera and asked, "What are you talking about?"

The man pulled a sheet of folded paper from his back pocket and handed it to him. "You don't know? These are all over the city."

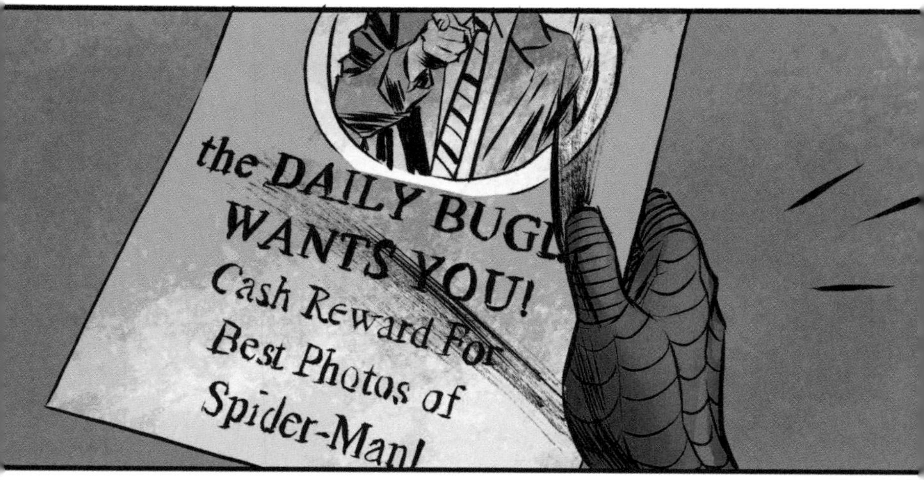
the DAILY BUGL
WANTS YOU!
Cash Reward For
Best Photos of
Spider-Man!

It was a flier with *The Daily Bugle* logo at the top and a picture of its famous Publisher J. Jonah Jameson, pointing like Uncle Sam in an Army recruitment poster. Beneath the image it read, "*The Daily Bugle* Wants You! Cash Reward For Best Photos of Spider-Man." And suddenly, Peter had an idea on how to save the apartment.

"These pictures are amazing! It looks like he's actually *posing* for you!"

In all their years together at *The Daily Bugle*, Robbie Robertson had never seen J. Jonah Jameson so excited over pictures and knew at once they found their winner. "How did you get these?" Jonah asked, as Robbie motioned for the other aspiring photographers to leave.

Peter Parker just shrugged his shoulders.

"I don't know, sir. Just lucky, I guess." Of course, Peter couldn't tell him the truth: He *did* pose for them!

"Poppycock!" Jonah shouted. "You make your own luck through hard work, Porter."

"His name's *Parker*," Robbie said with bemusement and placed a proud hand on young Peter's shoulder.

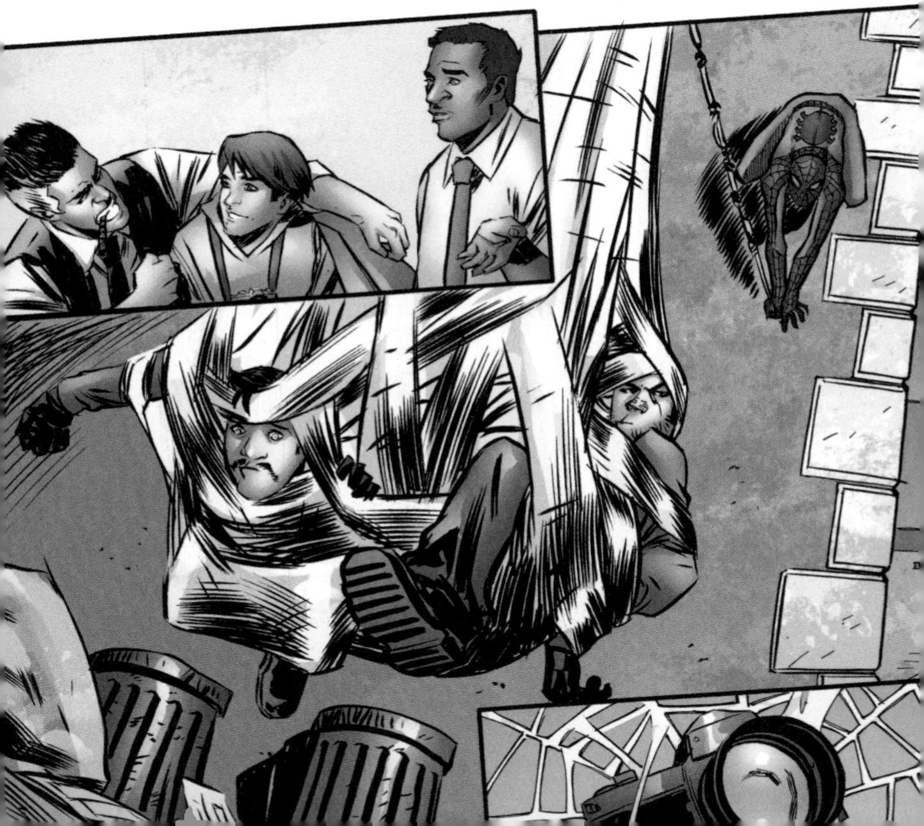

Jonah slammed the stack of photos down and walked out from behind his desk. He pulled Peter away from Robbie, and with an arm around his neck, he said to him in a very un-Jonah-like soft voice, "Forget the reward. How would you like to work for me?"

"Jonah! He's just a *kid*," Robbie said, not liking the idea at all.

"Freelance! For cash! What do you say, kid?"

It was out of Robbie's hands. Jonah and Peter both had the look on their faces that said they were up to no good.

And from that day on, Peter Parker was *The Daily Bugle's* anonymous staff photographer by day and patrolled the streets of New York City as a super hero by night. When danger called, he simply climbed a nearby wall, webbed the camera to it and set its automatic timer to catch himself in action. The next day, he'd deliver the pictures to Jonah and bring the money home to pay Aunt May's rent.

It turned out Willie Lumpkin was right: That old camera *was* worth something.

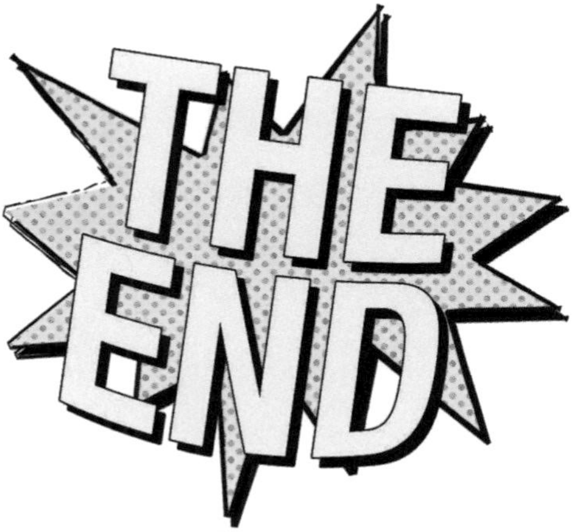
THE END

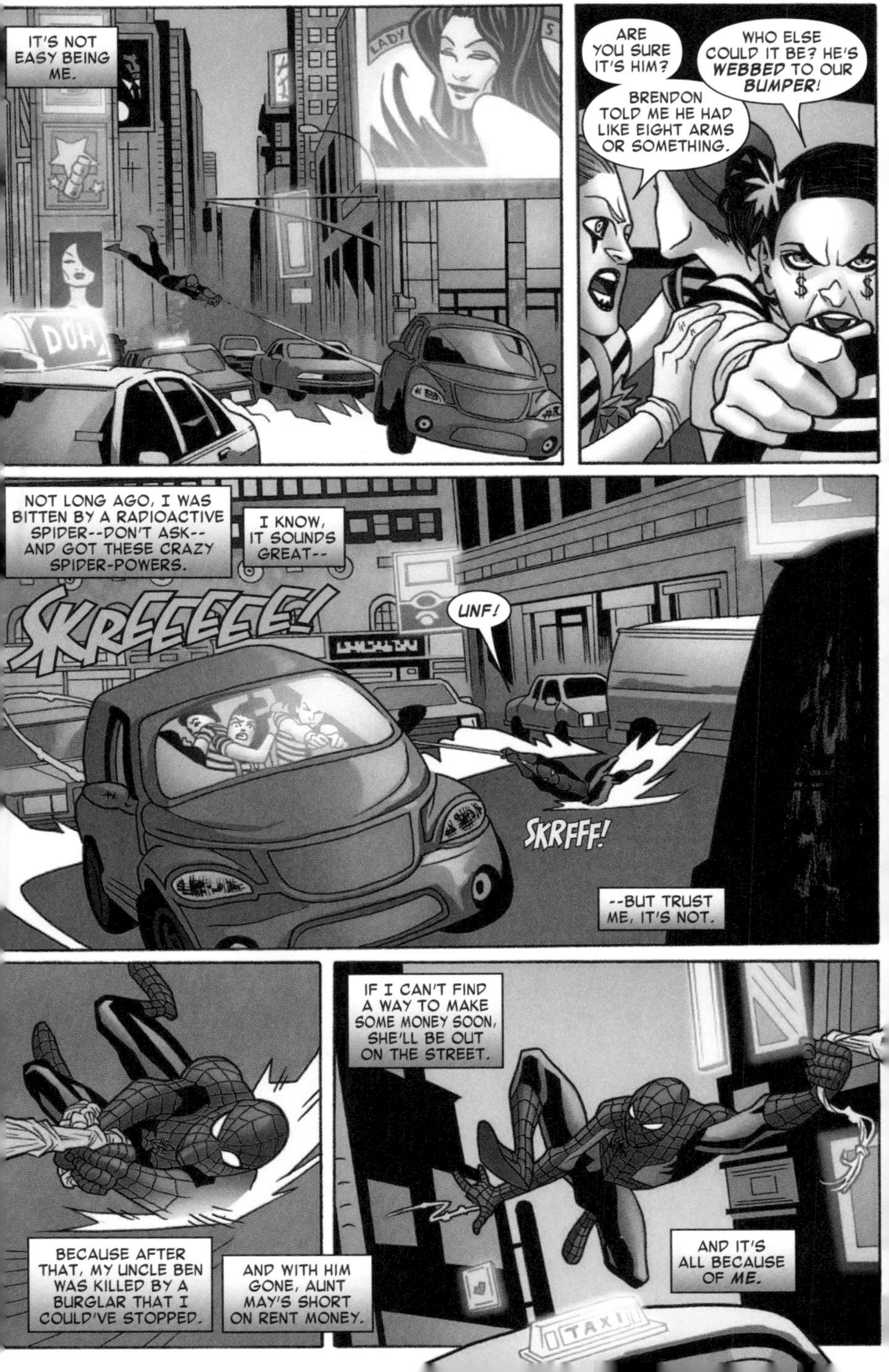

IT'S NOT EASY BEING ME.
ARE YOU SURE IT'S HIM?
WHO ELSE COULD IT BE? HE'S WEBBED TO OUR BUMPER!
BRENDON TOLD ME HE HAD LIKE EIGHT ARMS OR SOMETHING.
NOT LONG AGO, I WAS BITTEN BY A RADIOACTIVE SPIDER--DON'T ASK--AND GOT THESE CRAZY SPIDER-POWERS.
I KNOW, IT SOUNDS GREAT--
SKREEEEE!
UNF!
SKRFFF!
--BUT TRUST ME, IT'S NOT.
BECAUSE AFTER THAT, MY UNCLE BEN WAS KILLED BY A BURGLAR THAT I COULD'VE STOPPED.
AND WITH HIM GONE, AUNT MAY'S SHORT ON RENT MONEY.
IF I CAN'T FIND A WAY TO MAKE SOME MONEY SOON, SHE'LL BE OUT ON THE STREET.
AND IT'S ALL BECAUSE OF ME.
TAXI

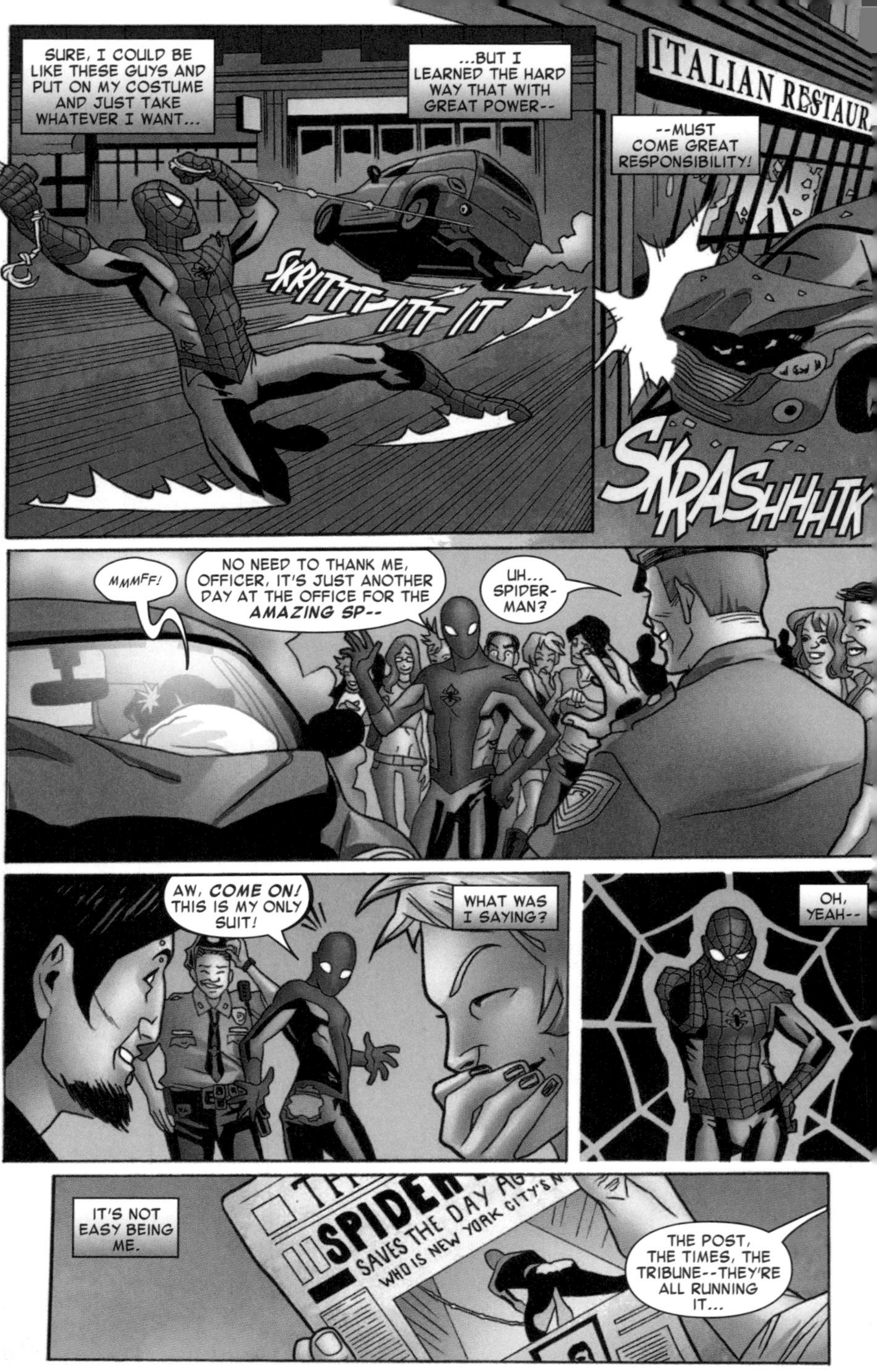
SURE, I COULD BE LIKE THESE GUYS AND PUT ON MY COSTUME AND JUST TAKE WHATEVER I WANT...
...BUT I LEARNED THE HARD WAY THAT WITH GREAT POWER--
SKRITTT ITT IT
ITALIAN RESTAUR
--MUST COME GREAT RESPONSIBILITY!
SKRASHHHTK
MMMFF!
NO NEED TO THANK ME, OFFICER, IT'S JUST ANOTHER DAY AT THE OFFICE FOR THE AMAZING SP--
UH... SPIDER-MAN?
AW, COME ON! THIS IS MY ONLY SUIT!
WHAT WAS I SAYING?
OH, YEAH--
IT'S NOT EASY BEING ME.
SPIDER
SAVES THE DAY AG
WHO IS NEW YORK CITY'S N
THE POST, THE TIMES, THE TRIBUNE--THEY'RE ALL RUNNING IT...

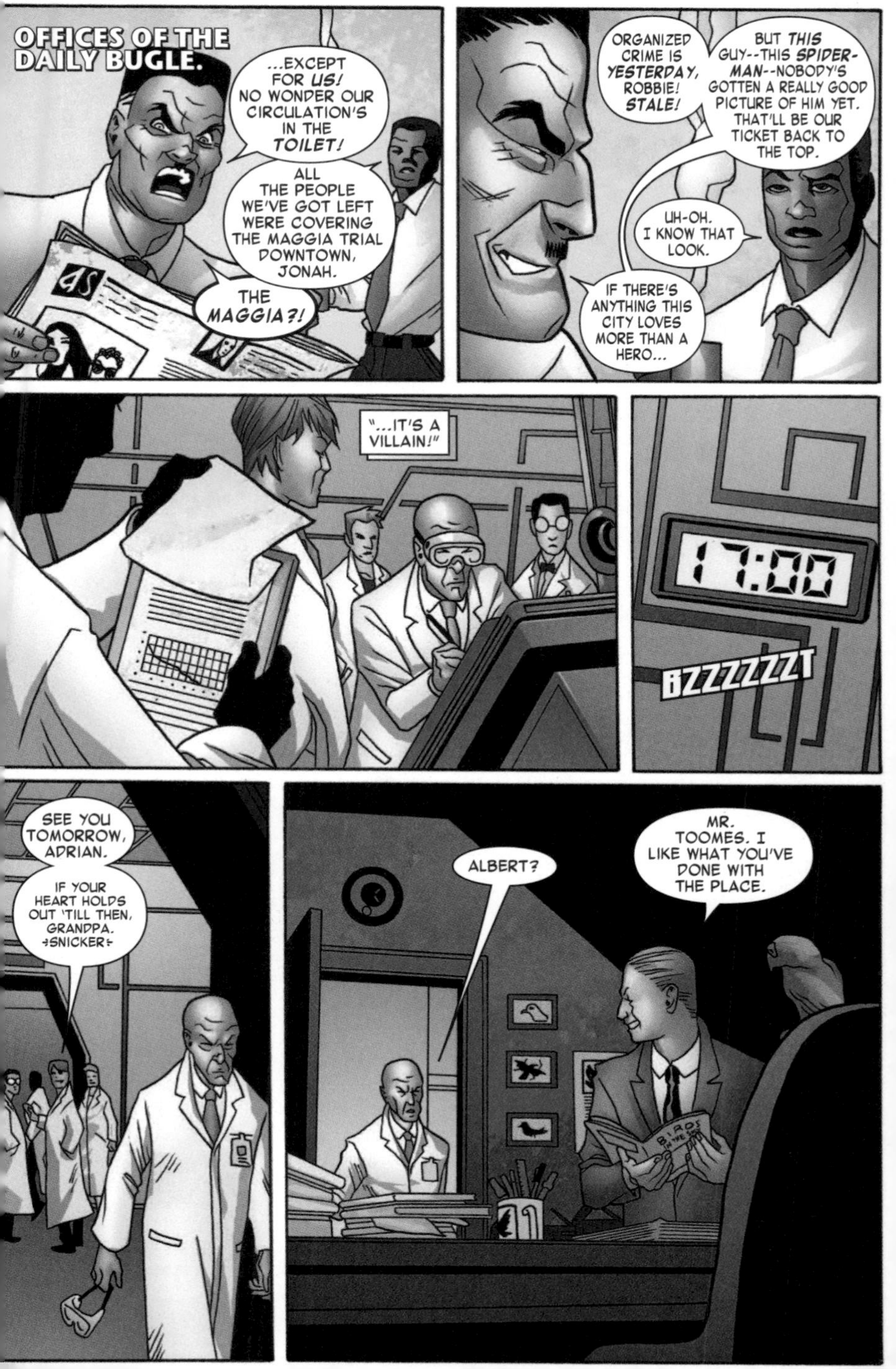
OFFICES OF THE DAILY BUGLE.
...EXCEPT FOR US! NO WONDER OUR CIRCULATION'S IN THE TOILET!
ALL THE PEOPLE WE'VE GOT LEFT WERE COVERING THE MAGGIA TRIAL DOWNTOWN, JONAH.
THE MAGGIA?!
ORGANIZED CRIME IS YESTERDAY, ROBBIE! STALE!
BUT THIS GUY--THIS SPIDER-MAN--NOBODY'S GOTTEN A REALLY GOOD PICTURE OF HIM YET. THAT'LL BE OUR TICKET BACK TO THE TOP.
UH-OH. I KNOW THAT LOOK.
IF THERE'S ANYTHING THIS CITY LOVES MORE THAN A HERO...
"...IT'S A VILLAIN!"
17:00
BZZZZZZT
SEE YOU TOMORROW, ADRIAN.
IF YOUR HEART HOLDS OUT 'TILL THEN, GRANDPA. ≠SNICKER≠
ALBERT?
MR. TOOMES. I LIKE WHAT YOU'VE DONE WITH THE PLACE.

NICE BIRD. WHAT'S HIS NAME?

HAR HAR. VERY CUTE.

NEPOTISM.

WHAT DO YOU WANT, ALBERT?

OKAY, MR. TOOMES, I'LL JUST GET RIGHT TO IT.

YOU'VE BEEN WITH THE MARSHALL CORP. FOR, WHAT, TEN...TWELVE YEARS?

THIRTY-SIX.

RIGHT. SO YOU KNOW THIS PAST YEAR HAS BEEN BAD. VERY BAD. AND IT'S MY JOB TO STOP THE BLEEDING.

THAT MEANS REPLACING THE OLD WITH YOUNGER, MORE EFFICIENT MODELS...

...INCLUDING EMPLOYEES.

WAIT--

YOU'RE *FIRING* ME?

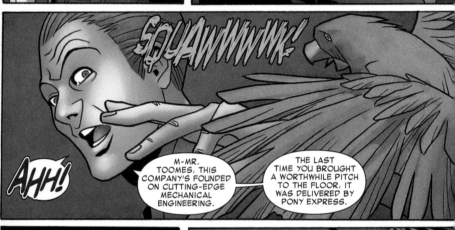

*SQUAWWWWK!*

AHH!

M-MR. TOOMES, THIS COMPANY'S FOUNDED ON CUTTING-EDGE MECHANICAL ENGINEERING.

THE LAST TIME YOU BROUGHT A WORTHWHILE PITCH TO THE FLOOR, IT WAS DELIVERED BY PONY EXPRESS.

WHAT ABOUT *"THE VULTURE"*?

Y-YOU MEAN...

...YOUR *BIRD* SUIT?

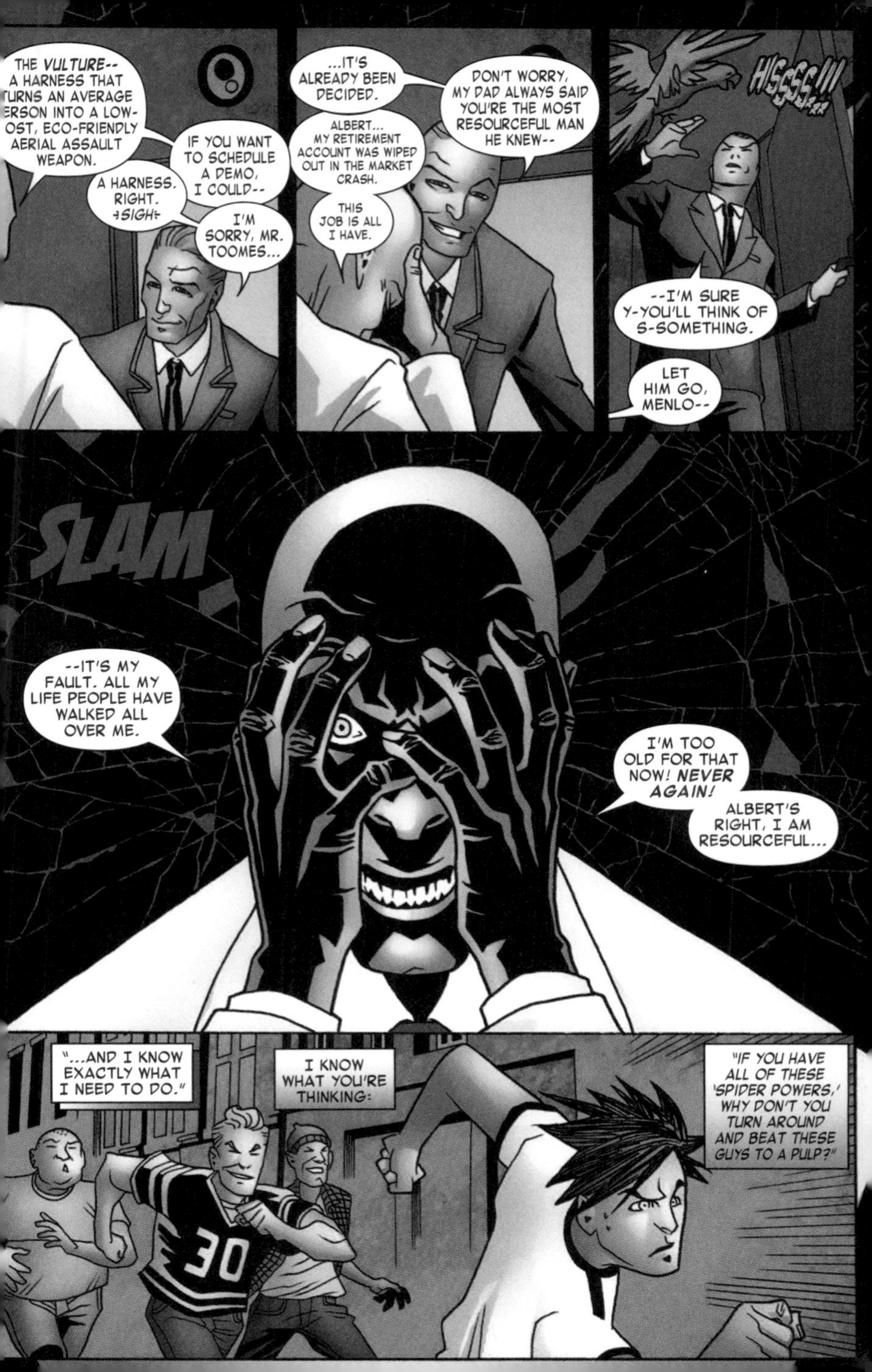
THE VULTURE-- A HARNESS THAT TURNS AN AVERAGE ERSON INTO A LOW-OST, ECO-FRIENDLY AERIAL ASSAULT WEAPON.
IF YOU WANT TO SCHEDULE A DEMO, I COULD--
A HARNESS. RIGHT. *SIGH*
I'M SORRY, MR. TOOMES...
...IT'S ALREADY BEEN DECIDED.
ALBERT... MY RETIREMENT ACCOUNT WAS WIPED OUT IN THE MARKET CRASH.
THIS JOB IS ALL I HAVE.
DON'T WORRY, MY DAD ALWAYS SAID YOU'RE THE MOST RESOURCEFUL MAN HE KNEW--
HISSSS!!!
--I'M SURE Y-YOU'LL THINK OF S-SOMETHING.
LET HIM GO, MENLO--
SLAM
--IT'S MY FAULT. ALL MY LIFE PEOPLE HAVE WALKED ALL OVER ME.
I'M TOO OLD FOR THAT NOW! NEVER AGAIN!
ALBERT'S RIGHT, I AM RESOURCEFUL...
"...AND I KNOW EXACTLY WHAT I NEED TO DO."
I KNOW WHAT YOU'RE THINKING:
"IF YOU HAVE ALL OF THESE 'SPIDER POWERS,' WHY DON'T YOU TURN AROUND AND BEAT THESE GUYS TO A PULP?"
30

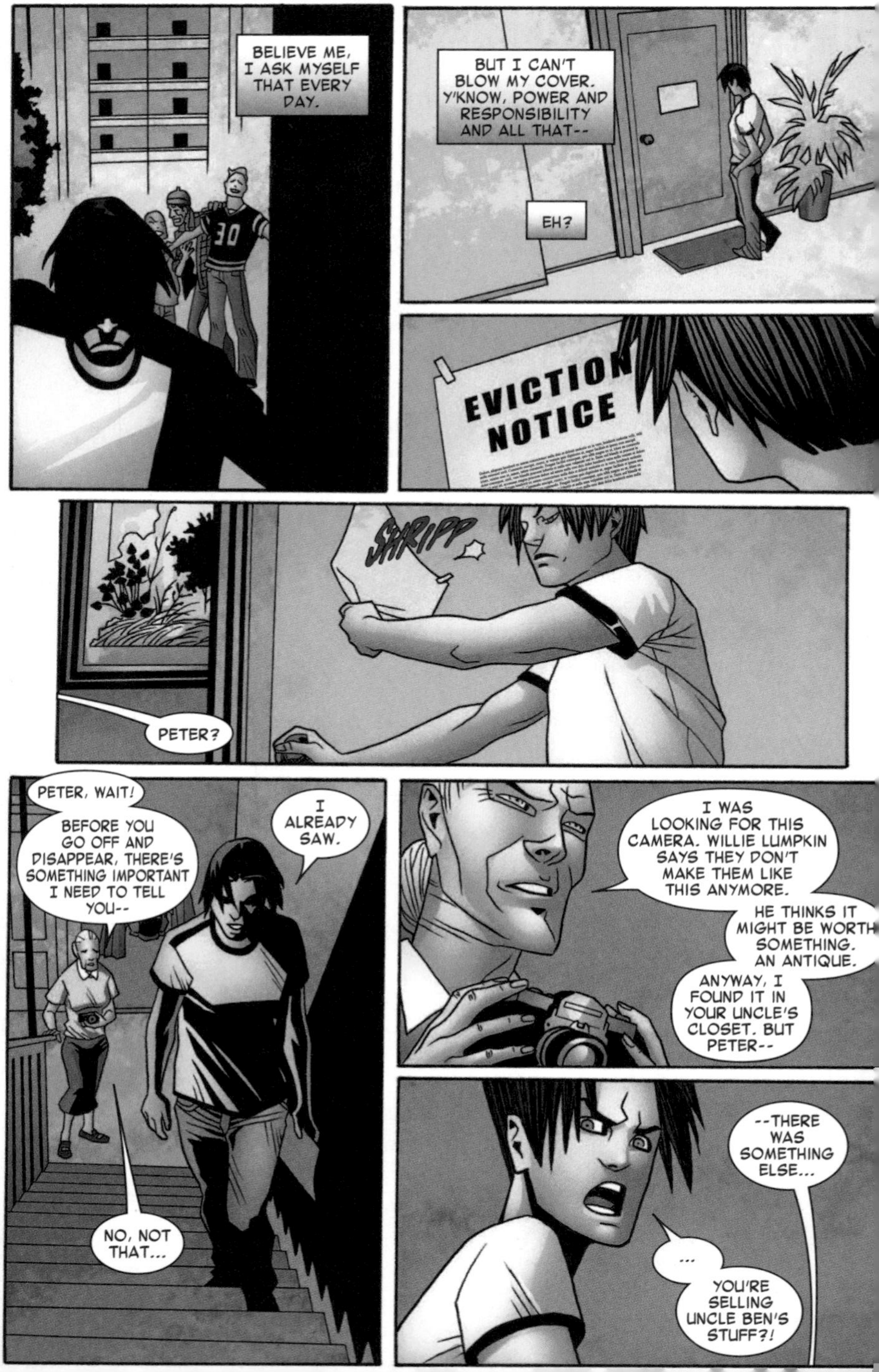
BELIEVE ME, I ASK MYSELF THAT EVERY DAY.
BUT I CAN'T BLOW MY COVER. Y'KNOW, POWER AND RESPONSIBILITY AND ALL THAT--
EH?
EVICTION NOTICE
SHRIPP
PETER?
PETER, WAIT!
BEFORE YOU GO OFF AND DISAPPEAR, THERE'S SOMETHING IMPORTANT I NEED TO TELL YOU--
I ALREADY SAW.
NO, NOT THAT...
I WAS LOOKING FOR THIS CAMERA. WILLIE LUMPKIN SAYS THEY DON'T MAKE THEM LIKE THIS ANYMORE.
HE THINKS IT MIGHT BE WORTH SOMETHING. AN ANTIQUE.
ANYWAY, I FOUND IT IN YOUR UNCLE'S CLOSET. BUT PETER--
--THERE WAS SOMETHING ELSE...
...
YOU'RE SELLING UNCLE BEN'S STUFF?!

PUT IT BACK, AUNT MAY! PUT IT ALL BACK!

PETER!

I KNOW YOU HAVE A LOT OF GUILT OVER WHAT HAPPENED WITH UNCLE BEN.

I DO *TOO.* I KNOW WHAT YOU'RE GOING THROUGH.

NO, YOU DON'T! YOU *CAN'T!*

THEN *TELL* ME!

INSTEAD OF STAYING OUT ALL DAY AND LOCKING YOURSELF IN YOUR ROOM AT NIGHT--

--TALK TO ME. MAKE ME UNDERSTAND.

I-- JUST... *PLEASE* DON'T GET RID OF HIS STUFF.

THAT'S WHAT I'M TRYING TO TELL YOU...

I FOUND THIS IN THE CAMERA BOX. A BANKBOOK FOR ONE OF UNCLE BEN'S OLD ACCOUNTS.

I CALLED THE BANK... IT'S STILL ACTIVE.

WE HAVE THE RENT MONEY, PETER.

THERE, THERE. EVERYTHING'S GOING TO BE ALL RIGHT. FROM NOW ON...

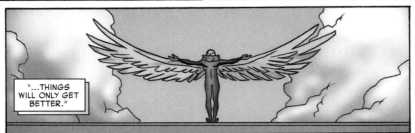

"...THINGS WILL ONLY GET BETTER."

**END PART 1.**

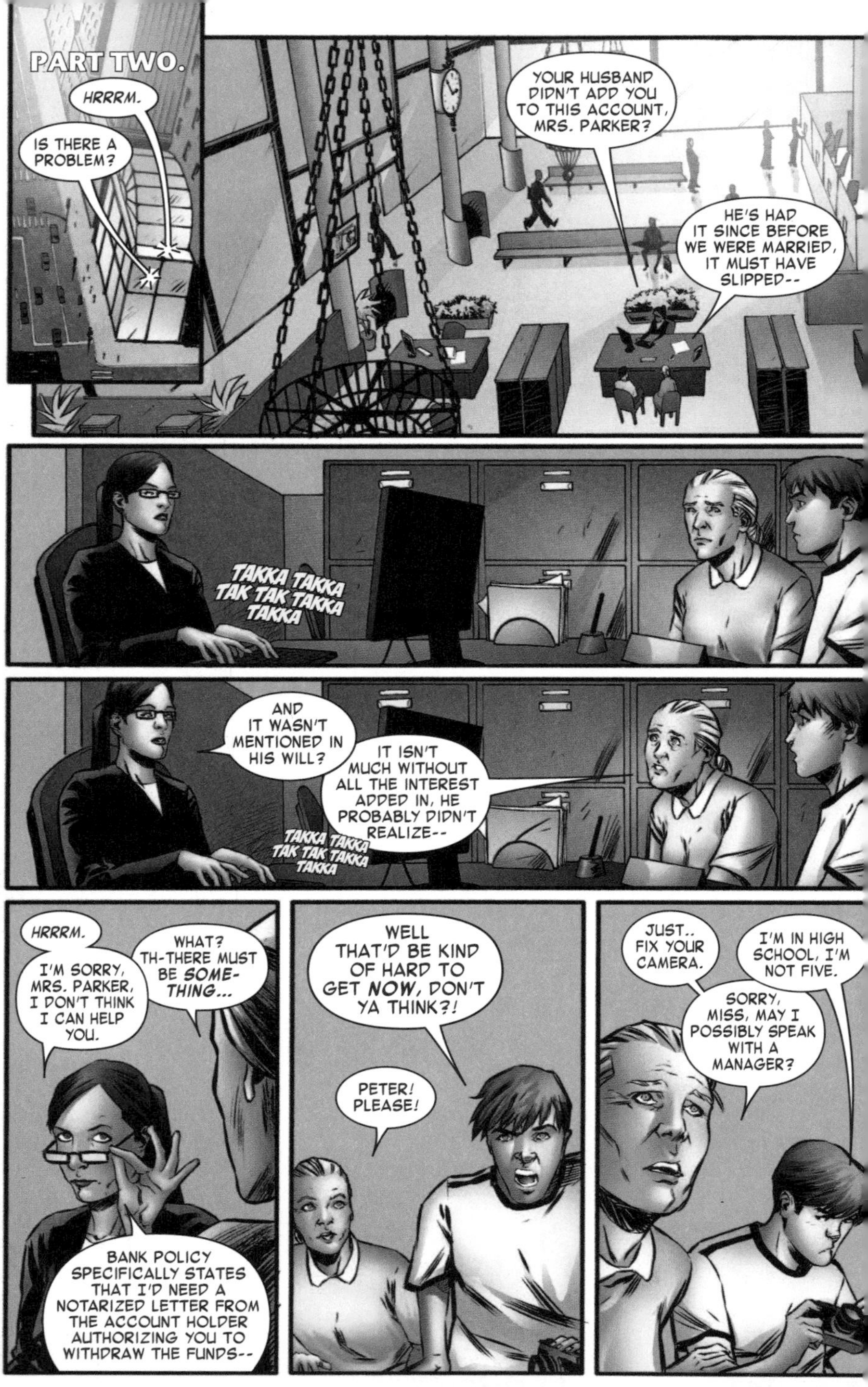
PART TWO.
HRRRM.
IS THERE A PROBLEM?
YOUR HUSBAND DIDN'T ADD YOU TO THIS ACCOUNT, MRS. PARKER?
HE'S HAD IT SINCE BEFORE WE WERE MARRIED, IT MUST HAVE SLIPPED--
TAKKA TAKKA TAK TAK TAKKA TAKKA
AND IT WASN'T MENTIONED IN HIS WILL?
IT ISN'T MUCH WITHOUT ALL THE INTEREST ADDED IN, HE PROBABLY DIDN'T REALIZE--
TAKKA TAKKA TAK TAK TAKKA TAKKA
HRRRM.
I'M SORRY, MRS. PARKER, I DON'T THINK I CAN HELP YOU.
WHAT? TH-THERE MUST BE SOME-THING...
BANK POLICY SPECIFICALLY STATES THAT I'D NEED A NOTARIZED LETTER FROM THE ACCOUNT HOLDER AUTHORIZING YOU TO WITHDRAW THE FUNDS--
WELL THAT'D BE KIND OF HARD TO GET NOW, DON'T YA THINK?!
PETER! PLEASE!
JUST.. FIX YOUR CAMERA.
I'M IN HIGH SCHOOL, I'M NOT FIVE.
SORRY, MISS, MAY I POSSIBLY SPEAK WITH A MANAGER?

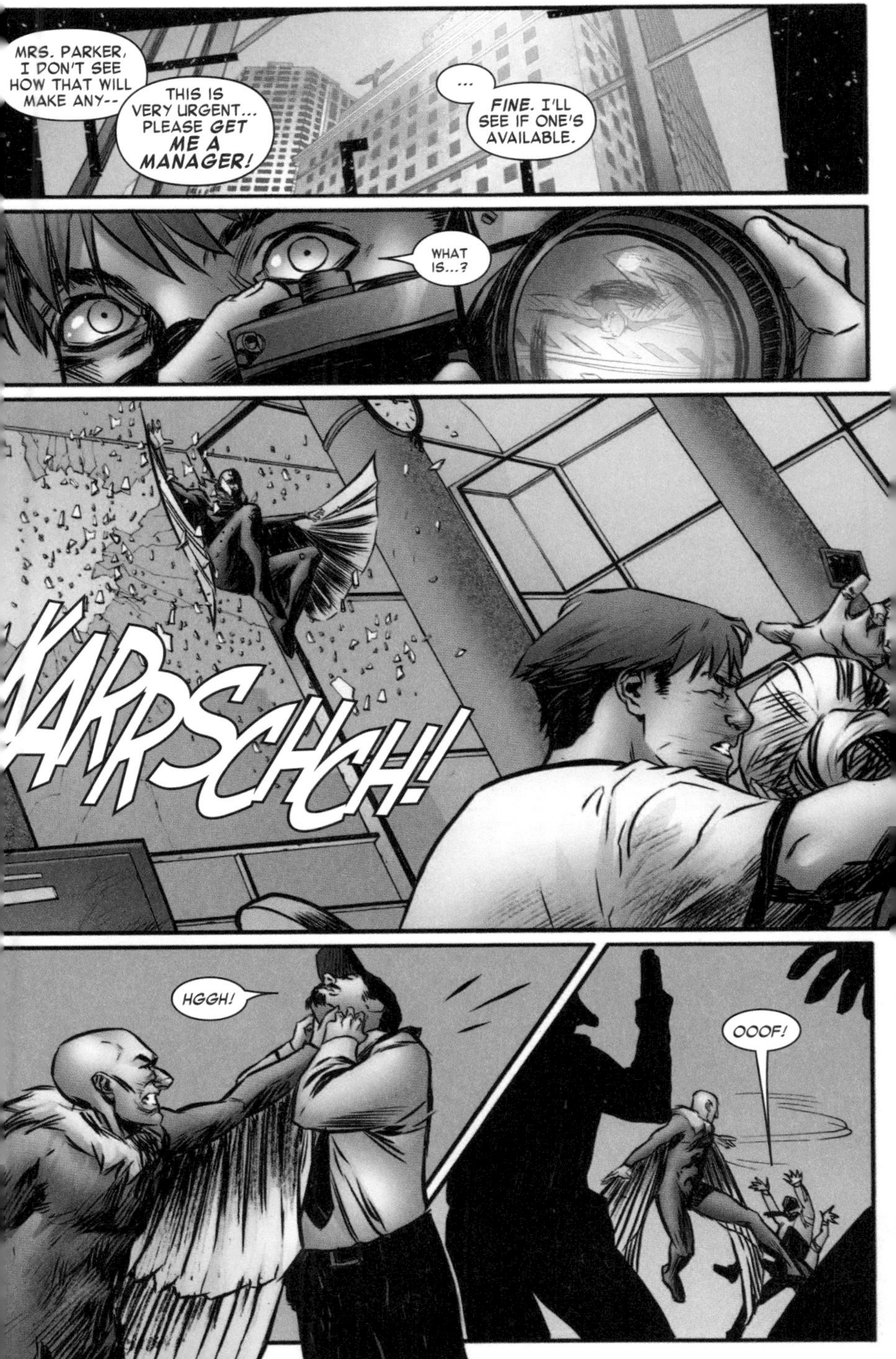
MRS. PARKER, I DON'T SEE HOW THAT WILL MAKE ANY--
THIS IS VERY URGENT... PLEASE GET ME A MANAGER!
... FINE. I'LL SEE IF ONE'S AVAILABLE.
WHAT IS...?
KARRSCHCH!
HGGH!
OOOF!

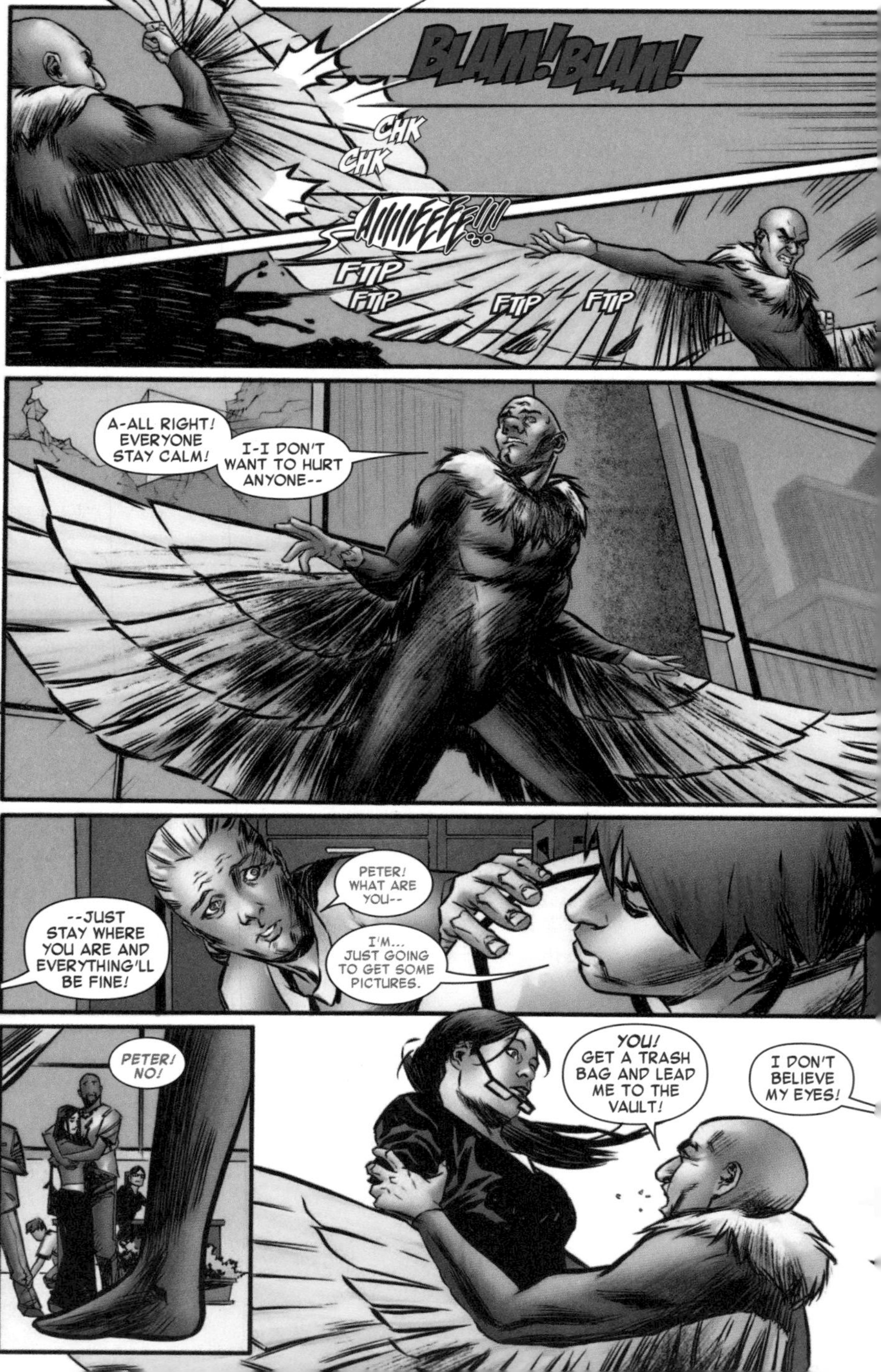
BLAM! BLAM!
CHK
CHK
AIIIIEEEE!!!
FTIP
FTIP
FTIP
FTIP
A-ALL RIGHT! EVERYONE STAY CALM!
I-I DON'T WANT TO HURT ANYONE--
--JUST STAY WHERE YOU ARE AND EVERYTHING'LL BE FINE!
PETER! WHAT ARE YOU--
I'M... JUST GOING TO GET SOME PICTURES.
PETER! NO!
YOU! GET A TRASH BAG AND LEAD ME TO THE VAULT!
I DON'T BELIEVE MY EYES!

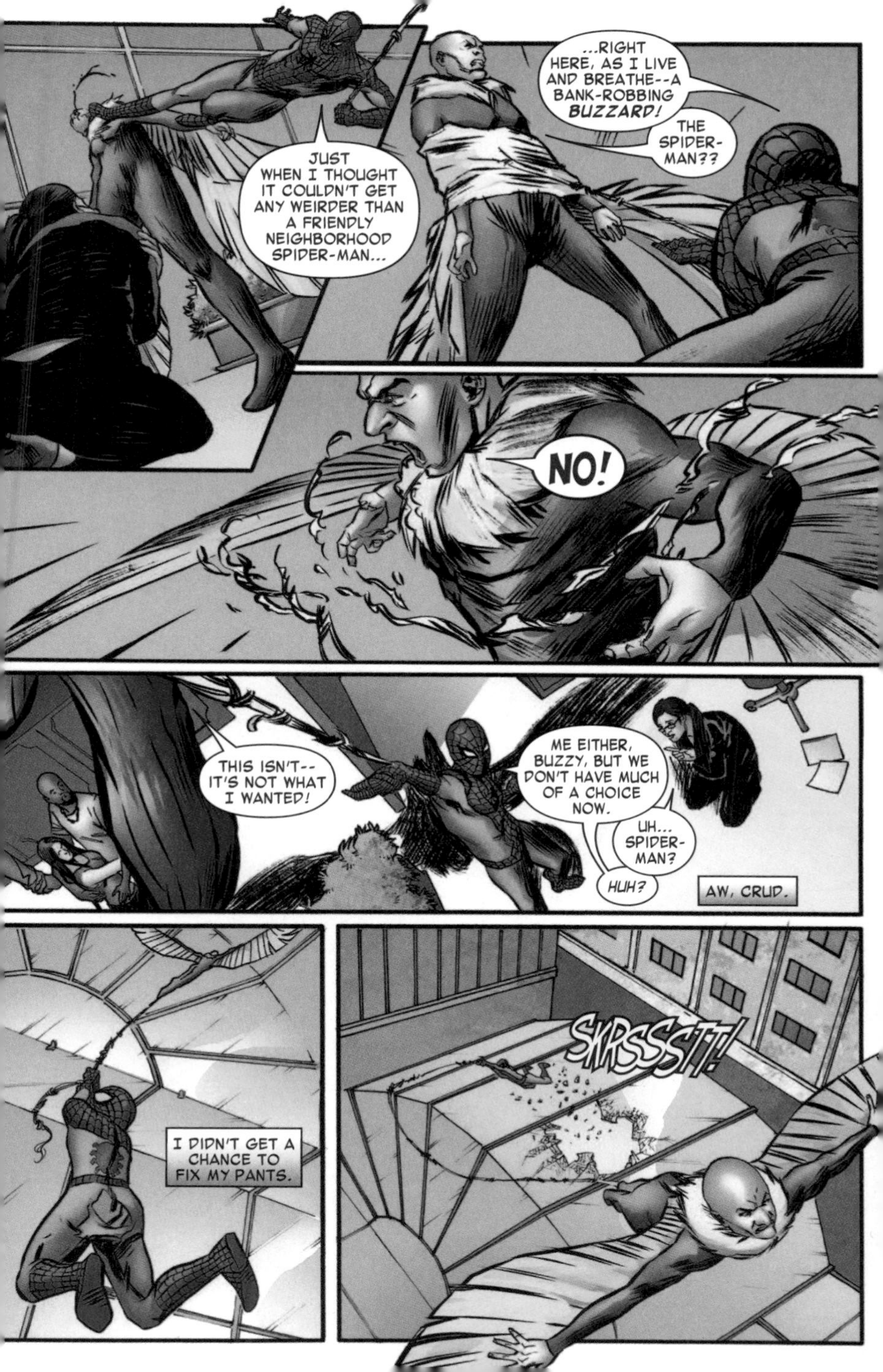
JUST WHEN I THOUGHT IT COULDN'T GET ANY WEIRDER THAN A FRIENDLY NEIGHBORHOOD SPIDER-MAN...
...RIGHT HERE, AS I LIVE AND BREATHE--A BANK-ROBBING BUZZARD!
THE SPIDER-MAN??
NO!
THIS ISN'T--IT'S NOT WHAT I WANTED!
ME EITHER, BUZZY, BUT WE DON'T HAVE MUCH OF A CHOICE NOW.
UH... SPIDER-MAN?
HUH?
AW, CRUD.
I DIDN'T GET A CHANCE TO FIX MY PANTS.
SKRSSSTT!

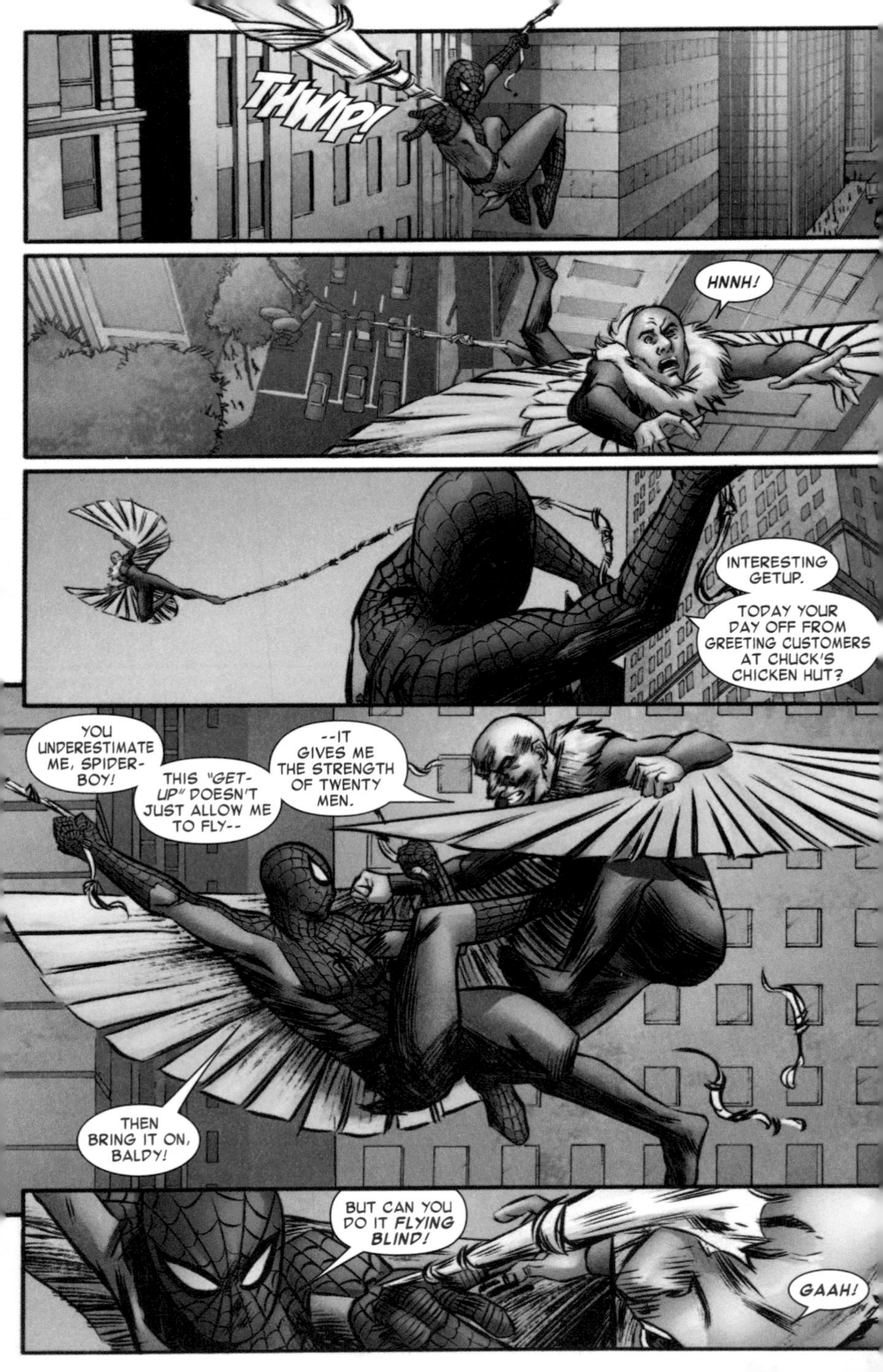
THWIP!
HNNH!
INTERESTING GETUP.
TODAY YOUR DAY OFF FROM GREETING CUSTOMERS AT CHUCK'S CHICKEN HUT?
YOU UNDERESTIMATE ME, SPIDER-BOY!
THIS "GET-UP" DOESN'T JUST ALLOW ME TO FLY--
--IT GIVES ME THE STRENGTH OF TWENTY MEN.
THEN BRING IT ON, BALDY!
BUT CAN YOU DO IT FLYING BLIND!
GAAH!

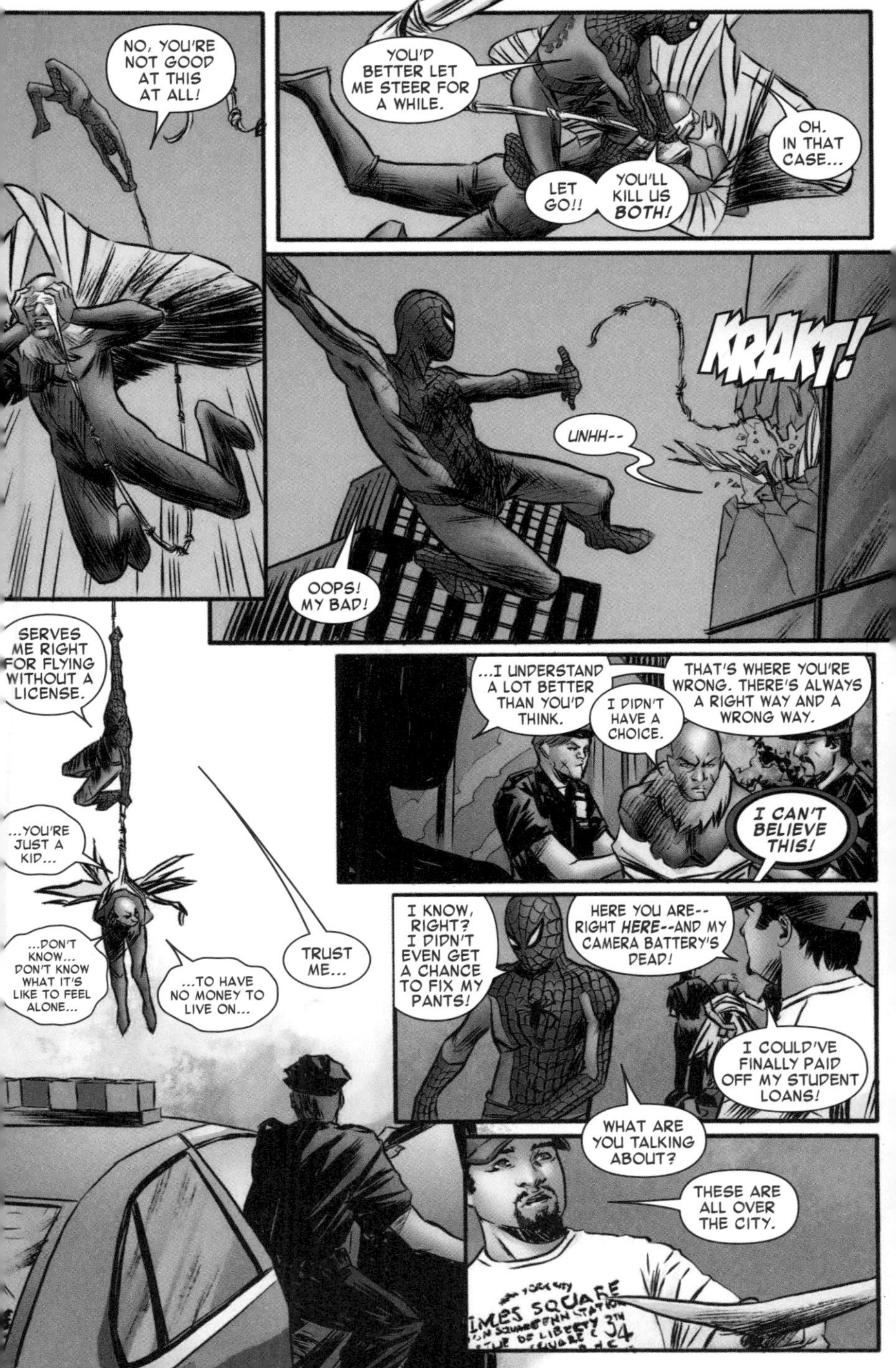
NO, YOU'RE NOT GOOD AT THIS AT ALL!
YOU'D BETTER LET ME STEER FOR A WHILE.
LET GO!!
YOU'LL KILL US BOTH!
OH. IN THAT CASE...
KRAKT!
UNHH--
OOPS! MY BAD!
SERVES ME RIGHT FOR FLYING WITHOUT A LICENSE.
...YOU'RE JUST A KID...
...DON'T KNOW... DON'T KNOW WHAT IT'S LIKE TO FEEL ALONE...
...TO HAVE NO MONEY TO LIVE ON...
TRUST ME...
...I UNDERSTAND A LOT BETTER THAN YOU'D THINK.
I DIDN'T HAVE A CHOICE.
THAT'S WHERE YOU'RE WRONG. THERE'S ALWAYS A RIGHT WAY AND A WRONG WAY.
I CAN'T BELIEVE THIS!
HERE YOU ARE--RIGHT HERE--AND MY CAMERA BATTERY'S DEAD!
I KNOW, RIGHT? I DIDN'T EVEN GET A CHANCE TO FIX MY PANTS!
I COULD'VE FINALLY PAID OFF MY STUDENT LOANS!
WHAT ARE YOU TALKING ABOUT?
THESE ARE ALL OVER THE CITY.

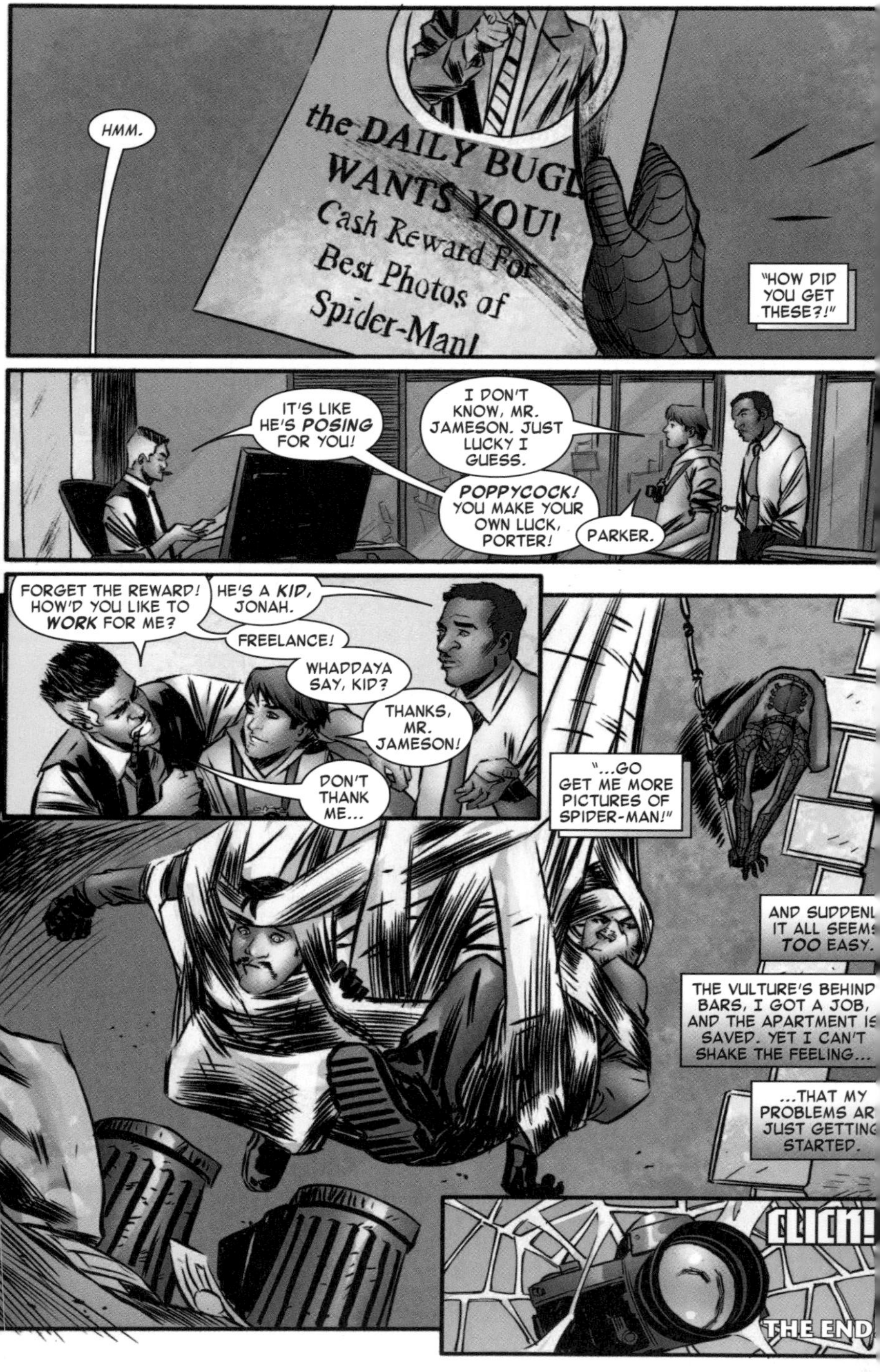
HMM.
the DAILY BUGL
WANTS YOU!
Cash Reward For
Best Photos of
Spider-Man!
"HOW DID YOU GET THESE?!"
IT'S LIKE HE'S POSING FOR YOU!
I DON'T KNOW, MR. JAMESON. JUST LUCKY I GUESS.
POPPYCOCK! YOU MAKE YOUR OWN LUCK, PORTER!
PARKER.
FORGET THE REWARD! HOW'D YOU LIKE TO WORK FOR ME?
HE'S A KID, JONAH.
FREELANCE!
WHADDAYA SAY, KID?
THANKS, MR. JAMESON!
DON'T THANK ME...
"...GO GET ME MORE PICTURES OF SPIDER-MAN!"
AND SUDDENL IT ALL SEEMS TOO EASY.
THE VULTURE'S BEHIND BARS, I GOT A JOB, AND THE APARTMENT IS SAVED. YET I CAN'T SHAKE THE FEELING...
...THAT MY PROBLEMS AR JUST GETTING STARTED.
CLICK!
THE END